dream in yourself

A collection of literary
works from Gallery 37

Edited by Quraysh Ali Lansana & J.M. Morea

Tia Chucha Press
Chicago

A special thanks to the Chicago Community Trust
for underwriting the 1996 literary programs at Gallery 37.

A special acknowledgement to the Prince Charitable Trust for their
generous donation in support of the Gallery 37 literary programs.

dream in yourself is a collection of poetry, prose and playwriting created by apprentice
artists in literary programs conducted in the Gallery 37 Schools Program in the Spring
and Fall of 1996 as well as the 1996 Summer Downtown Program.

Gallery 37 is a program of the Chicago Department of Cultural Affairs with
private funding provided through the Arts Matter Foundation,
a 501(c)3 not-for-profit organization.

Printed in the United States of America.

ISBN 0-938903-23-3

Book Design: Greg King

Cover Art: "Dream in Yourself" by Joline Finnigan, age 16

Published by:
TIA CHUCHA PRESS
A Project of the Guild Complex
PO Box 476969
Chicago, IL 60647

Tia Chucha Press is partially supported by the National Endowment for the Arts,
the Illinois Arts Council and the Lannan Foundation.

About Gallery 37

Gallery 37 is an award-winning jobs program that provides Chicago youth on-the-job training in the visual, literary, media and peforming arts. It has become an international model that has been replicated in 16 cities throughout the United States, and in Adelaide, Australia, and London, England. Initiated in 1991, this program was designed to provide meaningful employment and arts education to Chicago youth, and to increase public awareness of the arts as a tool for learning, critical thinking, building self-esteem and molding career choices. Gallery 37 has brilliantly captured the imagination of young people throughout the city, while transforming the Loop, neighborhoods, parks, youth centers and schools into workshops of artistic discovery. In its first six years, Gallery 37 employed over 6,000 apprentice artists in the Downtown, Neighborhood and Chicago Public Schools' After School programs, and has employed over 850 professional artists.

City of Chicago
Richard M. Daley, Mayor

Department of Cultural Affairs
Lois Weisberg, Commissioner

Gallery 37 Committee
Maggie Daley, Chair

Gallery 37
Cheryl Hughes, Director

The following organizations are literary participants in Gallery 37 activities:

Pegasus Players

Pegasus Players is the oldest cultural institution in Chicago's Uptown neighborhood, one of the most economically diverse communities in the city. While offering an award-winning season of plays to the general public, Pegasus has a deep commitment to audiences who have little access to the arts. In fact, Pegasus is one of the major providers of arts programs to the inner-city young people of Chicago through the Chicago Young Playwrights Festival program. Over 37,000 Chicago teenagers have benefited from the Festival since its inception ten years ago. This education arts program and writing contest for Chicago teenagers culminates with the original winning one-act plays enjoying a professional production as part of Pegasus' mainstage season. It is a program that involves teaching teachers to use play writing techniques as a continuing education tool to facilitate critical thinking and self esteem.

The Young Playwrights Festival has expanded to embrace several related initiatives. The theatre has been involved with Gallery 37, a hands-on arts program sponsored by the City of Chicago Department of Cultural Affairs for three summers, and last summer, the theatre ran its own play writing program through the city's Community Academy/Mentoring Initiatives Program. Pegasus Players created jobs for over eighty inner-city youths during the summers of '92 and '93 with their unique play writing and arts education programming through the Chicago Initiative Call to Action.

Guild Complex

The Guild Complex, an independent, award-winning, not-for-profit cultural center, serves as a forum for literary cross-cultural expression, discussion and education, in combination with other arts. We believe that the arts are instrumental in defining and exploring the human experience, while encouraging participation by artist and audience alike in changing the conditions of our society. Through its culturally inclusive, primarily literary programming, the Guild Complex provides the vital link that connects communities, artists and ideas.

Known for the high quality and diversity of its weekly literary readings and performances by emerging and established writers, the Complex often combines the spoken word with music, dance, video and the visual arts.

Tia Chucha Press, the publishing wing of Guild Complex, has established an international reputation for books of poetry that effectively combine poetry that matters and superb artistry. By publishing the best of emerging cross-cultural and socially-engaged poets, Tia Chucha Press has played a vital role in keeping alive the literary awakening that has been recently linked to Chicago, a poetry rebirth that has now swept the nation and many parts of the world.

CONTENTS

*"When members of a society wish to secure
that society's rich heritage they cherish
their arts and respect their artists. The esteem
with which we regard the multiple
cultures offered in our country
enhances our possibilities for healthy survival
and continued social development."*
　　　—Maya Angelou

Dear Friend:

We are pleased to present this second volume of literary works by Gallery 37 apprentice artists. This collection of prose, poetry and plays is a product of the 1996 Gallery 37 literary programs.

Gallery 37 was conceived as a program that at once addresses art education and youth employment, offering young people an opportunity to learn and apply essential work skills. Its success in achieving these goals is measured in the experiences of over 6,000 youth who have been employed at Gallery 37. The works in this anthology speak on their behalf.

The words of youth are powerful and thought provoking. They articulate the struggles and joy, the experiences and insights of urban youth. They are the voices of the future.

We thank the Guild Complex and Pegasus Players, who conducted the 1996 writing programs and trained our budding young wordsmiths to hone their thoughts and feelings into works of literary art.

Since its inception in 1991, Gallery 37 has brightened our city with hundreds of works of public art, such as benches that welcome travelers at the airports and murals that adorn our city streets. Its performing arts and literary programs have enlivened the city, producing prize winning plays and lively big band music. More significantly, Gallery 37 has unleashed the artistic talents of thousands of Chicago youth.

We hope you will take part in this exciting and continually rewarding program. Share the two Gallery 37 anthologies with your friends and family. Commission a work of art or purchase original artworks in the Gallery 37 Store. Through your participation, you are also contributing to the success of Gallery 37

Sincerely,

Maggie Daley,
Chair, Gallery 37

Preface

It is a tough time to be a teenager.

Not that it's ever been an easy phase to experience, mind you. It is possible to view the end of the twentieth century in the eyes of our youth. And what they have seen moves at break-neck speed and is utterly profound. In a world of drive-by's and super highways, our teens stand at a potentially dangerous intersection. Not only are they suspended in that place between adolescence and young adulthood, but this society demands they grow up and grow up quickly. I mean right now. Apprentice artist Sara Shirrell refers to it as a "breaking out of the clutches of childhood." It's inevitable, though it's not always stain free. Unlike so many Eastern cultures, we in the West have left our rituals of passage, and in many cases our children, to chance.

Gallery 37, in my mind, provides safe space for the evolution of thousands in search of themselves. Because it's not just about art. It's about responsibility, commitment and the desire to learn. Gallery 37 is about people-building.

dream in yourself is a book drenched in the notion of "keeping it real," as our youth like to say. It is a gathering of realities bound, like all of us, in a cover of shared experience. Think of it as a hymnal of raw honesty from minds and souls who may be closer to the truth than us "bigger kids." With few exceptions, every apprentice artist who completed a Gallery 37 writing program in 1996 is represented in this book.

There is a proverb from Zanzibar which reads "If the poet does not teach his song to the people, who will sing it?"

The songbook in your hands breathes easy, sometimes gasps for air, but never chokes. It is alive with all the simple melodies, complex refrains and dissonant chords of the Nineties.

On behalf of Glenda Fairella Baker, Eugene Baldwin, Tanya Baxter, Rolanda Brigham, Nick Eliopolis, Tsehaye Hebert, Tyhimba Jess, Emily Hooper Lansana and Diana Solis, let me say it has been a pleasure serving as choir directors.

Quraysh Ali Lansana, editor
Gallery 37 Teaching Artist

Introduction

The word inert' is derived from an earlier word: inart.' We understand inart to mean, literally, without art. It is difficult to imagine that any person would choose to be in a state of inartia. Yet, we have only to observe the world around us to understand that inartia, if not consciously contracted, has nevertheless slowly spread and affected a portion of our human family.

Gallery 37 then, in all its facets, is a potion, a prescription for inartia. I do not believe in inartia when I am there, for the tents and Cultural Center rooms are abloom with art, with creation.

Each year's apprentices offer me new challenges. If anything has changed in the five years I have worked at Gallery 37, it is that more recognition abounds. Repeat apprentices become veterans and spread the word to area high schools, and once-secretive playwrights and poets and story writers apply and come out into the light, thus revealing their secrets, reveling in their secrets, and may freely begin to thrive in a community of like-minded people.

To my apprentice playwrights, and to my colleagues on the teaching staff: this book is a salute to all of us, for ours is a healing profession. We shall overcome inartia.

If poetry is the art of brevity, playwriting is the art of long moments, pages of words. Publishing just three of our apprentice playwrights' full-length works would have taken most of the space allotted for our book. Therefore, we have excerpted a representative sampling of plays, and we have provided the reader with synopses of those we were unable to include. This is not a solution, but a plan of expedience. We congratulate all playwrights for their diligence, skill, and fortitude, for being willing to embark on a journey of discovery, even as, with all good journeys, they did not know the destination.

Eugene Baldwin, playwright
Gallery 37 Teaching Artist

Shadows

Listen to the words
The trees are trying to speak
in the sound of their sway

Taryn Michelle Harty

Is It Raining?

If you are a poet, you will
see clearly that there is
a cloud floating in this sheet
of paper.

-Thich Nhat Hanh

Does being a poet mean
That I see more than other people?
Does it mean that I walk through life
In a permanent hallucination?
The ink will run.

I am not as delusional as I look,
Merely lost in a dream-scape
Without windows or doors.
You can't see in,
I can't get out.

I am peering outward
From this cast.
This blanket.
It's on too tight.
The arms are too long
And tied behind my back.
I can't move them.

My page is in front of me,
Blank, yet undead.
I sense movement.
My shadow is moving on the page.
I am still.

It is raining
Heavily now,
And my thick red and blue ink
Streams down the page
Like fiery, bloody tears.
I have caused the rain.
I thought about it too hard
And it became true.

There is a cloud
Hovering over my page
And smearing my words.
The pen is alive
With definitions and explanations,
Breathing apologies.

Jennifer Clary

Quiet Enough to Listen

When I am quiet enough to listen, I hear this in my head: If it's a person, I hear their voice penetrating through my ears, traveling through the many nerve cells and delivering the message to my brain, where I'm the one who interprets what they are saying. Sort of like the Judicial branch, interpreting the laws that are made by the Legislative branch and are carried by the Executive. If it's another sound, for example a bird chirping, or a car passing by, I unconsciously pay attention to it. I know that the noise is there, but I really don't pay attention to it. It kind of enters one ear and exits another.

Patricia Perez

Dream State

When I am quiet enough to listen, I hear soft mellow hum-
ming noises that set off in my head and start me thinking
about the outside world, like birds whistling in the forest
or little tiny bugs ticking in air all over the world. It puts
me in a pleasant mood, as if I were in heaven and big white
beautiful angels were flying in all sorts of ways around me.
The sound is also like a clock before the final minute of a
time bomb. When I am quiet enough to listen, I fall into a
state of dreaming.

Rachel Ogundipé

Cleaning House

He remembered how his mother looked when his father had
left. He asked her what was wrong, and she started to cry.
His mother started to maniacally clean the house. Her tears
washed the windows and polished the television. Her tears
cleaned the bathroom and made the beds. When she was
done, the house was clean. The house was clean, and she
disappeared. She left for hours, and didn't come back until
morning. Jason wondered where she had gone. She had
bright red eyes, shiny from crying and a bright smile to dis-
guise the fear.

Erica Hieggelke

The Picture

There is a picture,
a pretty picture,
a female picture.

People walk by.
Some shake their heads,
some just stare.
This picture isn't perfect.

It is flawed in many ways.
People look and think they understand,
but what they think they know is all wrong.
Some laugh and call her names. She holds
her position without tears or anger.

At night she moves,
she talks, she cries,
she smiles, she dances,
she watches. She forgets
the words spoken about her and lets go. One day
she leaves. People wonder why, but only she knows.

Her picture will be painted over
and over again, until she speaks to
the people who hurt her.

Alison Ward

REALITY

Is she my mother?
Is she the meaning of the word?
People tell me I have to put up with her,
So I put my faith in the Lord.

Sitting down, watching Nickelodeon
Acting as if there wasn't a care in the world.
But when she walks in
Why does my stomach begin to hurl?
As if my body knows what's coming forth
By the tone in her voice.
I can't do anything. She's my mother.
If I only had a choice.

I'd walk to Texas,
Just to get away from my own screams.
But, the only time I get away
Is in my dreams.
There, ice cream is a nickel a scoop,
and I can be cowgirl, with metal on my boots.

I don't have a mother,
It's just me and my sister,
With our horses jogging down the path
Safe from mother's mean winter.

Nina Wiggins

Autumn

I saw many things
as Mother opened her wings to me,
I saw the dark sky
as I passed by
pretty houses
and some freaky buses.

There were houses for sale
and nature's tree getting pale
as they fell apart to start again and tell a new tale.

Autumn is coming,
But we are not happy, because bored we are becoming.
For trees, that change is a battle,
It is something that no one can handle.

It is something unexplained
that ruined our fun as it came.
Flowers and hard trees
lost their leaves
and the awful, silent wind
carried their seeds.

That chilly wind to us was brought
so that in it our fun could be caught.

Erik Ramirez

Natural High

Trees are shivering,
Because, it is too cold.
But they will survive.

The sun is leaving.
Now it is the moon's turn
to watch over this land.

The birds are singing,
Victory songs of heaven
The war's not over.

The Lord's love is here.
From the glorious heavens
made only for you.

A child shall lead them
Into battle today.
It shall be over.

Quietly sitting,
I keep my mouth closed tightly
as I watch the world.

Rather than judging man
Their souls gave me an image
Of what they were like.

Jamaal Webster

Untitled

Happiness surrounds the day
Even as darkness clouds the skies
Even as fog surrounds the bays
Even as millions around the world cry.
The music brings smiles to the faces of all
Even as many lives turn stale
Even as many face their mental walls
Even as many continuously fail.
The music takes us away from the stress
The music turns the dark clouds to rainbows.
The music is full of happiness
And allows us to hide from our sorrows.

Christopher Johnson

POEM FOR ANTHOLOGY

Time stands still on a Tuesday night
or simply
UNTITLED

On a Tuesday Melancholy
    stone set in my chair
    blankly gazing at digital
    seconds ticking away the
    Balance of the evening...
    the evening, night, lonesome
    a teasing...slight...longing
On a Tired Tuesday Low
    the soft yellow
    blanketing, lamp-light is
    Floating still...
    killing a stone gaze
    Isolation is perfected
    like a a single dull star
    obscured by clouds
On a Dull Tuesday Midnight
    the gentle beat distinct,
    the pitch softly blaring
    serenity
    like the last whispering
    silence
    but does not consume
    an empty shell of comfort
    like floating in a warm sea...
    thick rocking of
    heavy waves
    lets numb memories
    seep away as
    solitude swells

Eric Komosa

dead man stares out of his
fortieth floor window
at mothball martyrs of mystery
outside sun attacks pavement
where little lives are helplessly abandoned.

he is happy in his cage.

with each breath of air
his lungs are being cleansed
his insides are being reborn.

time is on his side.

pebbled walkways surround his confinement
sizzling sidewalks clatter with
uninvited sounds of industry.

dead man stares out of his
fortieth floor window
as the sky becomes hollow
rain begins to pour.

dead man stiffens his hand
gently grasps the windowpane
while a voice informs him,
"My friend you do not need to know
the number of spots on the sun."

Ann Janikowsky

Forever Waiting on Time

A clock represents time.
And we all know that
All it really says is tic tic tat.

We all wait on time.
While it moves at its own pace.
It hardly ever moves quickly
or in a haste.

Though it always moves
At the same speed
It sometimes seems
to be testing me.

I know that time
won't wait on me.
Though I often wait
for the time I want it to be.

I'm forever
waiting on time.
Sometimes for no reason
or rhyme.

A person keeps his own
representation of time
So I know that this is mine.

George Wilkins

I Am

I am a sister,
a person who is interested in music,
very shy and quiet,
friendly and kind.

I am very intelligent,
sophisticated,
a person of peace.

I am an honest person.

I am a person with a sense of humor,
I am a calm person who can succeed in life.

I am artistic.
I am an Aquarius.
I am 14 years old.
I am an auntie to a niece.

I am mysterious.
I am a daughter.
I am colorful.
I am European, Jewish and
a descendent of the Yukon Sioux tribe.

Virginia Hunt

SPIRITS

Cherokee, Iroquois,
Creek, Seminole,
Together.

Laughter of children.
The crashing, turbulent, roaring
sound of the drum.
Men chant.
Deafening, rapid
blustering of the
Great Spirit.
They chant.
They speak
for Mother Earth
and Father Sky
and for the sun
and its character,
and the animals
for their existence.
They chant.

Muneerah Askia

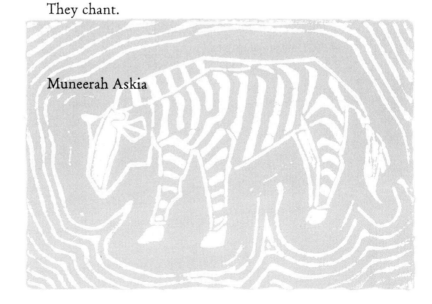

Silent Journey

When I am quiet enough to listen
I hear small leaves running across the clean, s
While little birds are flying against the dark a
I can see myself flying in the sky with my pet
Flowers blossom into different sizes and shap
while the earth is turning slow on its axis.
In houses and apartments people sleep
so the next day can come around.
People orbiting into space, finding a new plan
This is what I hear when I am quiet enough t

Fred Ogundipé

A Person Has to Have Magic

With a brush in hand
and a flare in mind

taking a step backward

bristling across the page
it leaps into a
blooming flame.

the brush dreams of
green and
finds red.

when I was
blank I was
disemboweled and now
I am covered and
complete.

dream of color
dream with color

paint stars on brick walls and
set fire to vinyl siding with the sunrise
while trees and bushes whistle
with wind.

dream in color
dream in yourself

tickle marble walls with
blue-born spheres and
caress concrete corners with
glowing nebulae

dream outside yourself
dream color

Michael Roston
(The eminently practical)

section two

Chicago, I hear you snore at night

opposite:
photo by
Jeffrey Stase, age 16

The Follower's Nation

When the leaders of ideas die or are killed
so dies the idea
and we are stuck in thought
like a fragmented sentence
going neither forward or back.

And everyone stands as if not knowing what to do
and then hidden agendas pollute the pure idea causing chaos,
which ruins it for everyone.
The ideas become polluted, too tainted to clean,
and the idea is lost in the poisons of humanity,
losing us and making us lose
what we want in the process.
Who we are is what we do
and when we know not what we are,
we in fact are nothing.
Like drone ants
bringing only nourishment for the queen
and ants with purpose,
we become meaningless
without purpose
waiting for another leader and their idea
to follow and fight to the death.

Jeanette Rusiecki

Should We Celebrate Columbus Day?

I do not think that Americans should celebrate Columbus Day.
Columbus, in my opinion, was an ignorant and hateful man.

He engaged in violent activities, killing robbing, and literally
raping Indians of land, rights, and their cultural way of life.
Anyone this intolerant, should not be remembered at all.

We are living in 1996. There is no reason and no room for ignorance. People were slaughtered by him and his men, mentally as
well as physically. Today we should be thankful that we have the
choice and the right to fight against different forms of hate.

Free your mind. Speak out. Educate yourself. Together we shall
be heard.

Sasha Sanapaw

No Corez Tus Raices/ Don't Cut Your Roots

As I stand in a supermarket check-out line,
I overhear a conversation between mother and daughter.

The mother says "Hija, que dice la muchacha?"
("Daughter, what is the cashier saying?")

"I don't know, Ma."

There are many cases like this one in the community I live in.
Latino teens refuse to speak Spanish in public
as if it were a bad thing or a shame.

I find this disturbing and an ignorant thing to do.
I know those teens speak Spanish at home.
They have to if their parents don't.
I think Latino teens should not forget
where they come from.
No matter what they do,
or how many years they live in this country,
or how well adapted they are,
nothing will ever change one's roots.

Maria Diaz

Abandoned House

There is an abandoned house across the street, and every
night when I sit on my porch, I feel someone staring at me.
I would love to go inside that house and see how it looks.
I wonder if there are nasty clothes lying on the floor, or if
it smells, or if it's burned. Maybe it was abandoned by its'
owner. Maybe homeless people live there now. It would
be interesting to go in and see.

Jennifer Small

A Place of Mystery in My Neighborhood

There is a place of steel and stone. It's an old movie theater on Belmont and Paulina. It has been abandoned ever sense I can remember. When I was younger, around seven or eight, it was a place of adventure and exploration.

Climbing the old rickety fire escape to the top of the world, I'd watch all the people go by, see downtown lit up at night, or just lie around looking at clouds. As I grew older, the place seemed to change. It was the summer before eighth grade, and this place of adventure and exploration turned into a place of excitement and mischievousness.

The goal of my friends and I was to get in and find something; I still don't know what. Breaking windows, prying doors, yet we never got in. Sometimes I look back and think that it's better just to imagine. Now that I'm a young adult, that old building made of steel and stone has turned into a place of first loves and fascination. Climbing on that old rickety fire escape to the familiar roof, has turned into a world of firsts. A world that is full of excitement, a world where anything can happen. I wonder when I'm old and gray, and drive by that building on Belmont and Paulina, what it will mean to me then.

Sarah Smith

My Neighborhood

My neighborhood is quiet
with big buildings,
small buildings,
apartments covered with pretty colors.
Old people, young people,
adults and children,
gays and lesbians,
people of all different cultures.

In my neighborhood
you can hear
birds singing,
dogs barking,
footsteps,
and talking.

What's bad
about my neighborhood
is the violence and gangs.

It's known as a peace–making place,
and not meant for violence.
If there were no gangs
in my neighborhood
it would be the best thing
for everyone.

Carmen Peden

Justice

I know Justice and his weakness
He couldn't stand erect
And project righteous rhetoric
That would glue – bind the mind
And suffocate the heart of broken words.

Make Justice question himself.
Justice unsure of what is right
And what is wrong;
So Justice is a whore
A whore that sold herself to the politics
And puppet masturbator's
Who would rather kill us
Than look at us prisoners of conscience
We are not innocent
In the eyes of our fathers.

Justice
Was civil rights?
But the more events of actual fact repeat
The weaker reality becomes
An ocean into a stream
Into drops of water.

She ceases to live
In my presence
Justice bleeds
I will not help it heal
I will let it die
To be born again.

Arthur Taylor

Gangs

How can you ask for respect
when no respect is given?
How can you try to be a leader
and yet always follow someone else?
While your families love for you
is slowly dying.
Your love for them is already gone.
You say you've got enough love
out on the streets.
But pulling a trigger
really isn't love.
Selling and feeding to your community,
what you yourself wouldn't dare take.
You're killing your own people physically.
But killing yourself more inside.

Rachel Jackson

Our Worst Enemy

Television is our worst enemy.
It tells us what we should think.
It absorbs us into a state of absent mindedness.

Our priorities wrong,
TV is on 24 hours every day,
every year for all eternity.
We need to recognize our true potential
and send the TV enslavers a message.

When we were kids
if you wore Pro-Wings tennis shoes
people made fun of you,
because TV said what was popular.

Television is our worst enemy.

Tony Marasas

Just Put In Front of The TV

Just put in front of the TV,
The child had no mothering.
The only parents she had
Were from Nickelodeon.

Jogging around with any man.
Ready to leave at the drop
Of a dime,
Or for that matter,
A nickel.

Broke out to Texas
With no forwarding address.

Kayde Barretto

YESTERDAY

Yesterday I could feel his body close to mine
  begging me to join his sexual dance
Yesterday he said he loved me
  as his unforbidden phallus pressed inside of me
Yesterday it felt good when he clinged tight to my body
  his warm breath breathing in my ear
Yesterday we had no protection, but we made love anyway
Yesterday I loved him
Yesterday I found him in bed with my best friend
  I trusted him
Yesterday I was diagnosed with HIV, and he was gone
Yesterday I got pregnant
Yesterday I was underage
Yesterday I didn't know what love was
Yesterday

Scenecia Curtis

On Garbage and Looking in the Mirror

And so he walks
With a crutch
In one hand
And a bottle
In the other
Speaking silently
to
      himself.

On the outside
Mumbling about
His surroundings,
The white man
That wouldn't let him pee,
and the little Ghost behind him
That tap
      tap
        taps
on his shoulder
and whispers in his ear.

He is our scape–
        goat
The one at which we can stare
And shake heads
Blame on everything
and never think
        twice
When in fact
We created him
Made society with have and have not's

and for you to be rich
                    healthy
                              stable
                                   and better,

He must be
              poor
                   sick
                        crazy
                        and beneath.

We look in disgust
At garbage
But never look
At the creator,
Because to do
              that
Would mean
                   to
look in the mirror and
see our own reflections.

Alyssa Coiley

Mrs. Hollywood

Her face is plastic
Her morals, elastic
living in this spastic
world of war
warped out codes
of conduct, modes
of behavior
false hope being her only savior
They don't save her, nothing saves her
Everything she stands for slowly depraves her
reduced to nothing more than a soul sucking fiend
from the trailer projects shelter squat
lower Wacker Drive from which she was weaned
wrapped in her 5 cent tinseled splendor
beat up heart no longer tender
underneath, the tinsel's tattered
shattered spirit worn and battered
spattered blood internally bleeds
as the sadists sow their seeds
scattered across the seamy avenue
(how much of her soul do you have in you?)

Onome Djere

To Live Out Here

I go to the park,
and what do I see?
I see a gang.

A gunshot flies
Past my head.
I take the time
To thank God I'm not dead.

I do not think
I can take anymore
Seeing the drug dealers
at the corner store.

The pressure gets worse
every single day.
It's not right
To have to watch
My back when I go
out to play.

I think about joining
a gang now and then.
But I know once I do,
It will just be the end.

I take as much as I can.
But to live out here,
you have to be a man.

Mark Saunders

Don't let them

Don't let them
take your circles
and make them squares

Don't let them
take your soul
and leave you alone

Don't let them
take your heart
and tear it all apart

Don't let them

Don't let them
treat you like a slave
and boss you around

Don't let them take
over your mind and
fill it up with dirt

Don't let them take
over your body and
put stars on it

Don't let them
shoot you and leave
your body on the
ground to die

Don't let them

Nicole Nathaniel

Remembering

I remembered, before I died,
that every day in the hood
niggas was up to no good.
And when I was strapped
I felt good.

I should have remembered that all my life
I've seen people fall
and they never got a chance
to fulfill their dreams at all.

I remembered that life ain't no game to play
It was do or die— that's the way.

I should have remembered that
living in the Ghetto ain't right,
dodging bullets everyday and night.

I remember that if you tried some bull on me
I woulda popped you as easy as a–b–c.
I shoulda remembered that if I live by the gun,
I'll die by the gun.

And if I don't live by the gun,
I'll still die by the gun.

Lindbergh Askew

Bone Thugz N' Harmony: A Review

The reason I like Bone Thugz N' Harmony:
Their music talks about the streets,
how drugs are being sold
and how people are getting killed, shot, and
raped.
They rap about their hood.

I like all of their songs because they mean something.
Some people don't like their songs
because they talk about drugs and smoking weed.
And I like the way they sing also.

Keisha Wills

The Road to Heaven
(An Original Gospel Song)

I'm on the road to Heaven
So Devil, you're not going to hold me back
I'm going on the right track.

I'm doing good now and forever more
I'm on the right track
So what would you hold me back for?

I'm on the road to Heaven
So please don't cry when I am gone
I won't be very long.

When I get there my troubles will be left behind
I will have peace of mind.

I will have joy – joy – joy up there in Heaven
My God will feed me till I want no more
I won't have to worry about being poor.

Because my Father is rich in houses and land
I'm going to Heaven, so give me a hand.

Falyn Shavon Harper

Dedicated to the members of the Poetry
Group of Gallery 37, 1996

Inside a glittering confession
breaking of the braces of childhood–
we lie awake in the night,
hearing, but never listening to the angry cries
and bitter screams of anguish.
We shake off the uneasy suffering
eating us alive and pushing us forth
into what lies beyond.
The guns forced, scraping down our throats
we are bound in a world unforgivable.
Inside and out of emotional boundaries,
we breathe our lives.
Escaping what is left of reality
into what is there for us in insanity

Sara Shirrell

Untitled

The door is locked
Education is the key
To open all doors

The plant is in bloom
The fields begin to appear
The door opens

The plant is in bloom
The landscape starts with a frame
The impatient field

Shelton Finley

Valley of Dreams

There's a place in the sky
past the moon and the stars,
past the sun and the clouds,
that's highlighted with pastel blues and pinks an

Like Easter
    reincarnated into a palace.

It whispers comfort and reassurance
to all those who pay a visit.

The door is a jeweled throne,
drowned
in diamonds and gems of every color and type,
that requires no key,
    just
        belief.

As soon as you set your hand on its knob, the
open and gently coaxes you inside,
    using no words.
And from that point on, all your worries, conce
problems are erased
    just
        like
            that.

This faraway place buried gently in the sky can
somewhere else, too--in your heart.
But
    it's up to you to enter the same jeweled doc

Kendra Walker

Chicago

Chicago, you gave me old women who sit on benches watching life
speed by in cars and trucks

Chicago, you gave me Midwestern accents which I cannot recognize

You gave me empty parking lots where only drunken crowds dare to
tread

You gave me children who, on crowded buses, clutch strangers' legs
in desperation

Chicago, you gave me windows from which mothers, wives, lovers
and daughters hang, waiting

You gave me apartment houses to which no visitors stray, thousands
of voices behind the newspapers whispering, projects

You gave me Dunkin Donuts, Taco Bell, McDonald's, Wal-Mart
and the Currency Exchange, neon signs which have caught a
million dreams

You gave me silence that is never interrupted by gunshots

Chicago, you gave me Belmont Avenue where teenagers peddle
dimebags to the likeliest customers

You gave me liquor stores where we escape with a ten dollar bill

You gave me a winter that bites and begs for recognition

You gave me the ignorant masses in khaki shorts and white T-shirts

You gave me an AM that is full of the ranting of the overprivileged

Chicago, every upper middle class child I have met in your hallways
had pale skin and I want to know why

Chicago, when you open your arms you have cartons of cigarettes,
plates of grease and old-name stores to sell

Chicago, you put strangers in cages at Lincoln Park Zoo and offer
them overpriced peanuts

Chicago, I can hear you snore at night

Chicago, you gave me supermarket aisles where arms in brightly
colored vests put a price on culture?

You gave me the faceless house at Ohio and Artesian where I
always return when I need food or sleep

Chicago, you gave me the cafes full of smoke and stores and cynics

Chicago, you gave me a sun that rises on your lakefront property
and sets by the faces of your forgotten children

Chicago, you gave me a downtown where no one stays after the
day's bread has been broken

Chicago, you gave me a Southside that cries at the richer, thinner
and northern of its frontier

Chicago, you know the names of your sports teams, but do you
know the faces of truth?

Chicago, when will you be worthy of the miles of train tracks that
scratch your face?

Chicago, will you take your whores when they are smudged and
swollen?

Chicago, did you want your immigrants only in the daytime when
their backs are bent with labor?

You gave the world jazz and blues and now you must convince us
that you still have ideas

Chicago, you paid for the dark alleys where the sleepless lie with
shattered glass and shattered hopes, now will you pay for the
graves of the souls you broke?

Roberta Medina

The Fever of Joy

opposite:
lithograph by
Lauren Klopack, age 17

Love & Hate

If love is a dream,
then I hope not to wake.
If love is confusion,
then let my mind shake.
If love is the sun,
then let it burn on.
And if love is God,
then let Him rule long.
If love is a fairy tale
do let me see.
And if love is a person,
please let it be me.

If hate is a fire,
then give me a pool.
If hate is a trick
then I hope I'll outfool.
If hate is a rhythm,
then I'll break the beat.
And if hate is a hunger,
I just won't eat.
If hate is a story,
I'll close the book.
And if hate is a vision,
I just won't look.
If hate is a power,
I'm stronger than he.
And if hate is a person,
I pray it's not me.

Iesha Bailey

Los Freaks

To be isolated in a world of hatred,
cropped into a group of differentiality.
To be sectioned off from life, and the world.

Why are we considered freaks?
We only want to make a point.

Why are we locked out of the world?
We only want to be original.

Los Freaks is what we're called.
To be brief, to be original, to be

Los Freaks.

La-Teesha Mitchell

Untitled

Flowers flowering in the day
their petals fall into the water
fading away...

Our hearts are like
the flowers flowering

Our love is like the
petals fading away...

Sophia White

I See the Stars Dancing

I see the stars dancing
In his eyes
The sun
In his smile
That lets the
Whole
World know

He's happy to be
With her

I stare from afar
With raindrops
On my cheeks and
Fog in my eyes

I am left here
In the rain
All alone
With no umbrella
To shield me

Debra Pagan

Love

what is love?
love is something that two
people should share
love is something that makes
you care
love is something that
shouldn't hurt
love is sharing every
passionate kiss
love is being intimate with
just one partner
love means overcoming
any type of problems
love is jogging down a
sandy beach
love is floating in the
clear night air
while holding hands with
not a single care
love is about trust and
honesty

Cvita Sawyer

Red Wine

Sweet and bitter,
Pours like moonlight
and swishes in my mouth.
Come be my red wine
You can pour on me
like the moonlight and
swish in my mouth.
Be my red wine
Sweet and bitter
Red Wine

Natasha Binion

Nausea

Cotton candy
and swirls of delight.
Excitement
flashed
the spinning sky.
I walked down
happiness with your hand in mine.
Our laughter
ringing
incessantly.
I teased your temptation,
you fed mine,
but we couldn't satisfy each other.
I forgot
the last time
I knew
or
felt
the fever of joy.
The world went
upside down
and rightside up
but we held on - together.

Susan Kurek

Purple Bridge

Laugh,
at yourself for being the fool,
for being who you are,
for being the comedian.
Laugh at me,
for responding to your stupidity,
for making up stories,
for dancing in the rain.
Like clocks ticking between air and space.
We danced together
Under the purple bridge,
Beneath the stars.
Counting one by one and craving the delight of infinity.
Over and over the song
played in my mind.
Someone sang a sweet lullaby
And put me to sleep resting in your arms.
I inhaled very softly-
Each quiet heart beat.
We sat there alone,
Dependent on each other.
Enfolded in the wind and sealed
In precious memories.
And if we listened very closely,
We could almost hear someone whisper,
"Goodnight, dear angels,
rest upon your fluffy clouds
and dream innocent dreams.
I am with you always, for eternity."
As I slowly opened my eyes,
There beamed a lustrous reflection
of our friendship, our faith, and our love.

It was you and I together,
Among the stars that we've wished upon
time and again.
You hadn't stirred as the new day ascended,
and I doubt you will remember the voice.
But I know that in love
You'll find strength and courage
To believe in you and I.

Lee Skruch

Untitled

I want to suffocate
your attentive blossoming eyes
with the piercing anxiety
burning in mine.
How would you reply
if I whispered into your
responsive ear
all you ever wanted to hear
that you will never
experience without me.
Come closer and bend down
slowly, no don't tremble.
I know that you've never
done this before,
especially not through me.
I won't warn you
about the hazardous peak
which strikes my resting
fury into devouring
your sensitive flesh.
You will remember the moist
scars, while others
will feel my trademark.
I'm imagining biting
your most delicate
core untouched by betrayal.
You pour your innocence willingly
into my hatred.
How fresh and beautiful you are,
not used to the swallowing
might of a thunderous creature,
that tore into my cherished purity
and relieved its condemning cruelty,

infesting my passion with
contagious revenge.
Laughing hysterically,
while sucking a path
through my poisoned blood
drowning the pleasure of new love,
for savages that you breathe for.
I'm breeding the lust of torture,
and spreading it within your
young, affectionate body
as you begin to worship the magnetic
destruction you now possess.
Fiendishly you scratch others
out of temporary vulnerability,
that gives to erotic brutality,
and trust liars like us.

Sylvia Pyrich

A small path through the woods.
Dark. Can't see ahead...

Your cold dead hands
hold me down
wrapped lovingly around
my waist.
You see yourself as my protector;
I see you as my obstacle.
As I feel my way
through this world,
you tell me what to expect.
So, I've seen this mystery before,
only through your bloodshot eyes,
and not my own.
I grasp and reach for hope.
You hand it to me.
I refuse, and hear you
say,
"You'll never make it without me...
Not without my help..."
But hold me back
with your cold dead hands.
You pull me up when
I want to cling to the earth
I've never felt before.
I yearn to see with my own
eyes.
To struggle through the darkness
and find my own destination which is
still unknown.
You may be able to tell me:
"You need me, I don't need you..."
But really, you need me

to carry out the dreams
you wanted to reach
but couldn't because you were
too weak.   Too fragile
to touch a thorn, to reach
the rose, lest
your hands get scratched.
And I, I am strong.
Stronger than you.
And therefore I hate
the cold dead hands
you wrap
around me, holding me up,
because I cannot learn
to rise,
until I have learned
to fall.

Marija Nikin

Mamma Blues

Yesterday I got in trouble.
Mamma, oh mamma, didn't stop yelling
Yes, indeed, I got in trouble yesterday.
Mamma didn't wanna stop yelling
My mamma yelled so loud
My ears started swelling.

After yesterday, I'm too scared to talk to my
mamma
I won't utter a word.
Nope, I won't talk to my mom
Not one single word.
For if I said something
She wouldn't like what she heard.

My mamma ain't that big though.
She's shorter than me.
Mamma really ain't that big.
She's shorter than me
But she's the only one right now
That can decide when I'm free.

Joann Vergara

Untitled

Listen
Follow up, it's all I ask;
See me not, for I am used.
You left me knowing, that I cannot see;
You left me giving, that I forsake.
Leave the scars, that I've been hiding.
Help the truth, that I see not.
Use my living, so I can fall.
Back my softness, so I can feel.
Set the point that I've been longing.
Let the fear feel my pain;
Let the spirit touch my soul.
Have the fortune bring my luck.
It's all I asked; to follow up.

Thuy Truong

Moments of Careless Forgetting

An excerpt from

Innocence
by Emily Schafer

Maybe now I can see them--as they were--then--more vividly than ever. I'm staring out this small perfectly rectangle-shaped airplane window onto the open O'Hare runway, and the memory materializes as an image, levitating above the grassy field, the painted pavement lines, the red lights lining the way.

All five of us are sitting around the low wooden coffee table in my basement, the soft dull orange carpeting beneath us. MTV percolates, but none of us are really watching. We're paying attention to each other, grabbing jelly-bellies out of a large bowl, fighting over the buttered popcorn-flavored ones, laughing. I remember the tacky silk flower centerpiece in the center of the coffee table. I feel the smell of the Air-Wick gardenia air freshener I sprayed before they came. Most of all, I remember their faces: Carrie, her pale flawless skin, perfectly applied black eyeliner and blackberry lipstick; Raven, her softly pleading brown eyes, and a dusting of copper-colored freckles across her round cheeks and nose; Crystal, her smooth features set in mocha skin, her small black eyes, two black stones; and Lucy, curly brown hair and skin pale and smooth as milk. Most importantly, the faces were all smiling, mine included.

There was a closeness between us then that I have never felt with any one else. We had all known each other since kindergarten, and had been an especially tight group of friends throughout junior high. Homework assignments, school dances, our first games of spin-the-bottle and truth-or-dare; we had been through it all together. We had just graduated, or had just been discharged is more like it.

We had told each other about the boys we liked, our first periods, our parents. Most of this information was exchanged at various times in my basement, our official hangout spot. And on this particular day in my memory, some really hard-to-swallow information had just passed between us. Yet somehow the passing of that information from Crystal's lips had caused its caustic quality to disintegrate, to evaporate into the air like the scent of the ersatz gardenias surrounding us. Crystal too was smiling with us, in a moment of careless forgetting.

I wonder if it was a real smile. It seemed real then. I didn't know that that would be the last happy moment between us.

Now I see that moment as the calm before the storm: it is as if we are on a gently rocking boat, unaware of the choppy waves to follow in our wake, when the storms of adolescence would kick into full swing. It was early June, the summer between eighth grade and that new prison camp--high school.

Now it is late August, four years later. All quiet in my section of the plane. Twenty minutes 'till takeoff, and then its good-bye Chicago. It will be a long, ten-hour flight. At last the sea storm has ended. We did not all make it through intact. One overboard; the rest abandoned ship, and scattered.

LIBRA: CARRIE

Carrie was the skinniest of us all. To me that was her most promi-nent feature. Like the scales of Libra, she had a physical balance, except that she really had nothing much to physically balance at all. Her movements were light, feathery; her skin fair; hair smooth and thick blonde. She was the makeup queen. Never a blemish did she show. She was flawless underneath all that makeup, but she'd freak out if she had to go anywhere without it. She seemed to make perfect sense to me back then.

Carrie was fun to hang out with. She was always happy, always get-ting over-excited about something, always making me laugh. In fifth and sixth grade the boys made fun of her because of her skinniness, but in seventh grade her body became fashionable, along with the clothes she wore on it. Everyone liked her then, and laughed at her way of getting all excited over nothing.

On that particular night in my basement with the jellie-bellies and the air freshener, she was the one who payed the most attention to MTV. She would look at the screen on and off, holding her gaze and widening her eyes when some long-haired, sweaty, muscular lead singer came on the screen. Then, since she was sitting next to me at the cof-fee table, she would clutch my arm and dig her long fingernails into my bicep, and squeal, "Oh my God, he's sooo hot!" Then I would laugh at her and tell her to calm down.

"He's just a person, he's not a god. He farts like the rest of us."

Then she would go into a hysterical fit of laughter and say that she didn't care, that she thought he was hot anyway. I remember her lying on her back on the floor, her slight chest heaving with laughter. Then she would sit up, fix all her silver jewelry back into place and giggle, looking straight at me. She was in balance. She was about just having fun, laughing, swooning over hot men in bands. She was fun.

SCORPIO: LUCY

For some reason the thing that automatically comes to mind when I think of Lucy is the color white. She seemed to always wear white and her skin was very pale. She had curly brown frizzy hair and a face that brought to mind the Swiss Miss girl. Her parents were immigrants from the Netherlands, and she was the least "American" of us all. She was never noticed by boys, but I always thought she was cute.

There was always something subtly desperate and grasping about her. Her mother had been suffering from emphysema ever since I could remember, and often when she was with us her mind would be at her mother's bedside. Sometimes she thought all our bantering, play-fighting and junior high giggling was stupid, sometimes she participated actively. But, like a scorpion, there was always something serious in her eyes, something cold in her movements.

At school she went unnoticed. She didn't speak out much, but when she did she stood behind her words as if she were supporting them with a marble pillar. Teachers and students alike thought she was a bit weird, always dressing plainly and simply, more for comfort than fashion, and speaking more like an adult than any of us. She got good grades, but usually developed hateful relationships with teachers. The hate was hers, it was her poison that she injected just underneath the skin of others. Once she decided she hated someone, that was it. She hated them forever. The teachers feared her, knowing about her home situation and the "problem" behavior it might bring about. She sensed their uneasiness and loathed them because she felt it had no merit, and it didn't. She never caused any trouble in school.

When Carrie was on the floor that night, laughing, Lucy hit her softly and said sarcastically, "Get up, ya freak!" Carrie puller her down with her and Lucy succumbed to laughing along.

CANCER: RAVEN

Raven had freckles, bright red freckles that stood out on her cheeks and nose, that matched her dark orangey hair. Her freckles stood out, and she stood out as well. She was an arguer, a loud-mouth, the devil's advocate. She had verbal crab claws. In grade school, when I would step out for a bathroom break and slowly walk back down the hall to my classroom, her voice was the one that could be heard the loudest, the furthest down the hall from the classroom. She would barge in on conversations and make an argument out of nothing, insisting that she was always right.

Sometimes Raven would tell me about her mother, about how she would always put her down for any little thing. I found that, after I listened to her, Raven could be very sweet. She would show me the tenderness in her that the crab had buried in the sand. This is why she was part of our group, she could be likeable and kind if you just paid her a little attention and let her have her say.

Raven really held on to us, treated us like her safety rope, like we mattered. It sounds cruel, but she wouldn't have had any friends at all if it weren't for us. We weren't part of the perky-breasted, flirtatious, tight sweater-wearing cheerleader crowd, and none of us were one of those icy-quiet wallflowers. We were the in-between girls. And in the seventh grade, it was definitely the best place for us to be. We had each other and needed nothing more.

GEMINI: CRYSTAL

Crystal had the prettiest skin color. She was half Puerto Rican and half Philippina, making her skin a light mocha. Her features were very well-defined, her body athletic. She played on the basketball team at Hawkeye Park near our neighborhood. She was pretty good friends with her teammates there, but it was us she told her story to that night in my basement.

I remember feeling first a great shock, then sadness, then anger, then admiration for her when her story came out. I had always admired Crystal for her athletic abilities, for I had none. Plus, she was confident, always seemed to have it together, never intimidated by anyone. It seemed as though nothing could break her down. Except this.

I don't remember how we got on the subject, but somehow we did, and somehow Crystal started to tell her story. Crystal had, at one point, begun to realize that she could vividly remember being in first grade and being in third grade, but she couldn't remember anything in between. She asked her mother about this, who told her that the summer before Crystal was to enter the second grade she took her to Puerto Rico for Crystal's grandmother's funeral. They stayed with Crystal's grandfather the whole summer.

Crystal and her mom slept in the guest room, which was separated from her grandfather's room by the bathroom. Crystal first remembered the funeral, seeing her grandmother in what she thought was a strange type of bed. She remembered wondering why everyone was watching her sleep, kneeling down in front of her, but not waking her up. Gradually, she remembered her grandfather's house and the room she slept in with her mother. According to Crystal, the rest came back to her like a rushing flood.

First, she remembered the sound of the running shower every morning. Her mother would always take long showers. Too long. A few weeks after the funeral her grandfather caught on to this routine. There would be creaking faucets, the water splattering on the ceramic tub, her grandfather's footsteps through the bedroom door, the sound of his hand clapping tightly over her mouth, the unzipping of his pants, his grunting as he broke her in half, the same way he almost broke her legs in half as he pried them apart. After he left the room, she was left on the bed, crying into her pillow, grabbing onto her mother's nightgown left on the bed and holding it up to her face to get comfort from the smell of her mother. When the faucets creaked again, the splattering water subsided, and her mother came back in the room in her white bath robe, Crystal would pull the bedcovers over her and pretend to still be sleeping. This happened repeatedly the rest of her summer in Puerto Rico. Funny what the mind can erase and uncover again.

This she told us as we sat around my coffee table, which was empty except for the tacky silk iris centerpiece. We were silent for a moment suspended in time, and then Crystal spoke:

"He's dead now. Just this week we found out. I figure I don't have to keep it a secret anymore. I told my mother about what happened. She didn't say much about it, but she decided that we don't have to go back to Puerto Rico for the funeral. I'm never going back there again."

"Good for you, girl," Raven said.

Then somebody said something and somehow we all started laughing, welcoming comic relief.

"Jellybeans, anyone?" I was trying to lighten up the atmosphere a bit more. This was supposed to be a party, and thirteen-year-olds can't stay dead serious for long.

I went up to the kitchen to get the candy. While I was there, somebody turned on the TV, and when I came back down Carrie was already drooling while a music video played.

We forgive men so quickly.

An excerpt from

Savannah
by Jonathan Farr

It was the summer of 1860, during the early start of the civil war. In the bustling city of Savannah rich, middle income and poor people showed how peacefully each class could live together. Savannah was a port city. Many sailors came to Savannah and saw the city's wealth. Savannah's ports were the largest in the south. Many clippers, schooners, flat boats and rowboats. Sailors traded fine linen and gold with bales of cotton. Tobacco was one of the easiest trade items. People also bought ships at the ports, while others came just to interact with the sailors.

The scorching hot summer of 1860 brought the fear of drought to all farmers' minds. Trees began to look like weeping willows, in desperate need of water. Cotton and tobacco fields, the south's main source of currency, began to die. Many farmers found it hard to support their families.

Small ponds and creeks began to dry up. The birds and other animals left their once permanent homes in search of water and food. Many fish died for lack of sufficient nutrition.

Many people died of heat exhaustion. People were getting sick from scarlet fever. Slaves could not perform the tasks of working in the fields due to the heat. Savannah needed rain very badly. People began to drink the water from the ocean. Salt and other impurities caused chemical reactions and many people died from the water.

Wealthy plantation owners built many mansions on the northern side of the city. Everyone knew who lived in the large estates. Cotton, wheat and tobacco fields surrounded many mansions.

Each plantation housed a large number of slaves. Most slaves worked in the fields. Others worked in the houses as cooks, maids, gardeners, horsemen, weavers, doormen, coachmen and bakers. Each plantation had 50 slaves or more.

Saxton's Manor, one of the largest plantations in the city, had a small lake right next to its cotton and tobacco fields. It also had many flower gardens. Rose gardens with narrow paths all leading to the sculpture of David, grew on the north side of the house. Hybrids and daffodils were on the west and east sides, while the fields were two miles south of the house.

Saxton Manor had 200 slaves to farm the 40 acres of land.

Christopher was the oldest slave, at thirty-five. Christopher was a field slave who was promoted to manservant. Matthew, Christopher's brother, was a doorman. The two brothers were the oldest and overseer to the slaves. If there was trouble concerning the slaves it was they who would try to solve the problem.

The house was three stories high with three marble pillars supporting the balcony in front of the house. Fine white linen draped the windows. Shutters were on each side of the windows. The house also had a balcony extending over the rose gardens and sculptured bushes. There were two cherry oak doors standing side by side. Each had a golden lock and knob, which showed the extent of the Saxtons' wealth. Many fine paintings lined the entrance hall of the house. A white marble floor with a staircase led to the second and third floors. A replica of the Birth of Venus was painted on the ceiling.

Thomas Saxton, owner of the estate, was a wealthy man who built ships for a living. He owned one of the largest shipyards in the south. His wife, Kelly Andrea Saxton, died while giving birth to their only child, Kathryn. After his wife's death, Thomas became cold and hated all doctors, for the doctor failed to save his wife from death. He was cold and angry toward everyone except his daughter. Thomas felt that he could not love anyone else other than Kelly, so he avoided other women as much as possible. He also felt that women had no business in men's affairs so he did not take his daughter with him to the docks. But she'd sneak down to the docks alone, whenever she had the chance.

Young Kathy Saxton was very fond of her father. She never had any man in her life, other than the cooks or slaves. Based upon the gossip that she heard from the other girls and women, she believed that all men were dogs. Kathy Saxton was only sixteen but, she thought that she had seen, heard and done everything.

During this summer, Kathy decided to make more friends. So, when an invitation arrived inviting her to a ball honoring Lord Anthony, she asked her father for permission to attend.

" Father, can I please go to Sir Anthony's ball Saturday night?"

"You can go to your beloved ball, but, I will not be accompanying you."

" Father, I am happy to go, but I would surely like for you to come with me."

" I cannot attend. I have business to take care of."

"You work too hard! You should take the time to meet someone."

" I have made my mind up. I will not go."

" I'm going to wear the dress that you gave me yesterday."

" What dress? I gave you no dress Kathy!"

" Father you gave me a green gown with golden bows on it yesterday. You bought it yesterday."   Thomas was stunned.

"Yes, I did give you a dress, didn't I?"   Kathy ran to her bedroom and pulled a light green dress from her closet.

At the ball, she met the Governor John Frank Jenkins. Governor Jenkins was concerned about the war. " I'm so scared that the Union troops might be heading for us. I still don't think our militia can stand up against them.!"

" Don't worry about them," said Captain Avery Johnson, confident in his troops. " Our troops could go against the whole army and not lose anyone!", he bragged. Kathy had a question but she preferred not to say it aloud. The question kept bugging her until she finally said, " Excuse me sir but just if it so happened that our troops can't hold the Union soldiers, what are we to do?"

" Didn't I just say do not worry!" Captain Johnson said harshly. Kathy ignored the comment and turned around to see a man's eyes sparkle at her. Maybe his eyes didn't sparkle, maybe it was the light shining in his face. For that one moment, she knew he was looking at her and for maybe just that moment, she actually liked it.
    Kathy walked over to the man and said, " Hello!, My name is Kathy Saxton of Saxton's Manor."

" Why yes, you are the daughter of Thomas Saxton, owner of the largest shipyard in Savannah! I already know who you are."

"Yes Sir that is me, but what is your name?"

" Lord Edward Williams The Second, of Williams Manor in Fredrickston, England. " he said. " I too own large shipyards of my own in London, Paris and Boston. " I am here to by a shipyard for sale here that my friend told me about on his visit to Savannah. The gentleman selling it is supposed to meet me here at one - thirty for the final price.

But why does my stay here makes you so curious?

Kathy looked at the wall, then at him.

" I am wondering if my father just might be selling the shipyard and the ship we are building."

" Do tell me where I can reach you?, " he asked.

Kathy starred at him.

"You already know that."

Near the end of the party all of the guest were given silver shovels to dig inside a sandbox in search of rubies, diamonds, emeralds and pearls. Kathy only found two small diamonds, ten giant pearls and sand in her shoes.

When Kathy returned from the ball her father was waiting for her.

" How was the ball?, " he asked.

" Oh, it was wonderful father. "

" Did you meet anybody? "

" Yes. I met this man named Edward Williams. He is from England and he came here to buy a shipyard. " I find it very strange. Who would sell a shipyard when the war is going on? Especially when the South needs ships? Father, do you plan to sell the shipyard? "

" Let us not talk about this tonight. You need rest and we will finish this conversation in the morning, " he answered harshly.

The next morning Kathy woke up with a start. When she looked up her father was looking down at her. He looked happy.

" Kathy, I have some very good news. I just made one million dollars! "

" That is wonderful, but how? " She asked.

" I sold the shipyard to Lord Edward Williams. "

" How could you do this to me? You knew I wanted the shipyard! How could you have done this without my consent! I hate you! Get out of my room now! "

Thomas grabbed her wrists just before she attempted to slap him. He threw her to the bed and yelled, " Don't ever say those words to me or you will be beaten. Lord Edward has taken the liberty in joining us for tea. Come down to meet Lord Edward when he arrives, and try to act natural. Do not embarrass me, or I'll tan your hide. "

When Kathy went down the stairs, her father told her "Remember, if you embarrass me, I will hurt you. "

When Christopher opened the door, Lord Edward stepped into the room.

" I adore the way you've decorated the house," he said.

"Why thank you, Sir Edward. Please won't you join my daughter and I for some tea in the drawing room. Right this way please. "

When they reached the drawing room, Kathy instantly sat away from her father. Edward was uncomfortable, because he felt some tension in the room, but preferred to say nothing. Kathy decided to break the silence.

" So you're the slime that stole my shipyard. "
Thomas shot her an icy look.

" Please excuse my daughter's behavior. I know I've taught you better than that."

" Excuse my outburst Lord Edward, I did not mean to take such matters out on you...no, I take my apology back. You men are all the same. Lying, greedy, dogs and think that you are superior to women. "

Thomas was furious. " Go to your room, for you will have no tea!"

Edward then said " Thomas, please, its okay. Do not worry about it."

" I won't let my daughter talk to an English gentleman like that."
Thomas said sternly. " She will be severely punished. "

The next day Kathy saw Edward at the docks. Her father had indeed punished her, for she had a black eye. Edward came to her and said " I wish I could have done something about what happened to you yesterday. My God! I wish I had done something instead of being so noble. Instead of being an English snot. "

" Don't blame yourself. I should have never said those words to you. It was not your fault, it was mine. I wanted the shipyard, and I thought it would belong to me when my father passed. I didn't mean to take it out on you."

" Do not think about it. I know about that clipper you and your father are building. Why don't we finish it, and I will race you for control of the shipyard. If I win, I gain control. If you win, you gain control. But where to race I do not know at the moment. Where do you suggest Kathy?"

" England! " she exclaimed. " That is to where I'll race you. "

" Alright then, it is a deal. When your ship is ready we will sail at dawn. Your crew against mine."

An excerpt from

Butterfly

by Yadira Lemus

"Damn it, get out of my way!," Sequoia hissed. She was extremely late in picking up her friend, Roslyn. Ros had told her to pick her up at exactly 6:15 p.m., or else her parents would try to force her to stay and eat dinner.

Sequoia shot a quick glance at the digital clock on the dashboard. She was half an hour late and she still had a while to go. Gripping the steering wheel tightly and clamping her teeth to her lips, she sped up as the light turned yellow.

"Gotta make the light!" she yelled. She zipped through the intersection. Loosening her grip on the wheel and letting out a hard whistle through her lips, she smiled nervously. It was 6:47 p.m.

"I am not hungry!," Ros wailed. She roughly pushed her plate back and shot up from her seat. She turned to go, but her father caught her wrist sharply.

"Roslyn, you apologize right now, missy!," her mother spat. Ros turned to her father and stared. Her gun steel grey eyes bore into his face like hot coals. He sat there calm and patient. His tiny, ferret eyes were hidden behind thick, bottom of the bottle glasses; they perched heavily on the bridge of his nose. A look of concern and fear swept over his face in a wave, then faded away. He lowered his eyes and cleared his throat after some time and spoke in a rusted, powerful voice.

"Do what your mother says, sweetheart. She went through a lot of trouble to make you dinner. Least you can do is thank her and apologize for your harshness."

Defeated and betrayed, again, Ros faced her mother, who was across the table tapping her foot on the worn linoleum floor. It reminded Ros of a time bomb. "I'm sorry, mother," she spewed, "thank you, though..." she lowered her eyes and hissed under her breath, "bitch." Hoping that she didn't hear her, yet masochistically hoping she did. Unfortunately for Ros, she did.

Her mother rushed around the table to Ros' side. She let a small, tight smile crawl eerily across her face. Her nostrils flared and a thick, bluish vein profoundly popped out on her forehead. Her eyes opened wide in their sockets, like looking down the barrel of the gun. They were hued that dark pitch of gray.

"What did you say to me girl?," she growled. Ros could hear the building, yellowish, gunky phlegm blanketing her mother's voice. Her mother's smile twisted into a snarl. Spit and snot struck Ros in the face as her mother began to rage. "You stupid good for nothing. Get out of my face!"

The screaming and the spitting ended with a thunderous crack from her mother's fist connecting with Ros' cheek. It was 6:47 p.m.

Sequoia slammed her foot on the brake. A stop sign. Her breath came in rapid and shallow chunks. She felt lightheaded and dizzy.

"I'm hyperventilating," she whispered. She told herself to calm down, it was just one more block. But it was no good. She suddenly felt sorrow and hurt overwhelm her. Fear swelled into a thick ball in her chest. She had to find parking, quick.

The street was empty. A cool breeze tossed the fallen leaves around; scraping them along the concrete with a clatter that echoed down the block. Her heart beat furiously within the cavern of her chest. A gust of wind swallowed her whole; running up her bare legs and burrowing up her shirt. Tepid fingers ruffled her short crop of bleach blonde hair gently.

She sucked in a hot drag off her cigarette, then harshly spit it out. She didn't park far, yet she was out of breath and tired. No, not tired, but exhausted. She trudged up towards her friend's house and pulled the gate back. It let out a painful groan. She looked back down the empty street and stared angrily at the sidewalk, the black asphalt street, then she looked up into the sky. The dark, forlorn sky that gently sighed for her with it's deep blue eyes. She looked back at Ros' house. It, too, seemed to sigh for her.

"Dear god," she breathed as she laboriously climbed the steps. It was going to be a long night.

Before Sequoia could even knock on the door, Ros' mother opened it.

"Hi there, sweetie," she purred. Sequoia returned the plastic, laffy taffy smile and leaned over to kiss her on the cheek. She could smell the dank, mustiness of sweat on her neck. It clung to her like a leech. Sequoia shivered. She knew that scent a little too well. It had the pungent stink of hate and madness merging into one.

"Come in and have a seat. Ros will be down in a minute," a thick voice called out.

She stepped inside. "Thanks, Mr. Meyers. How've you been?," she mewed. The air in the room swirled densely around Sequoia and drowned her. It was smothering.

"I've been fine, honey. Working a little too much, though. How've you been? And your dad?" He placed the newspaper neatly on his lap, and peered at her from his thick glasses.

"We're both fine, thanks. Will you excuse me, though." she hesitated, "I'm gonna run upstairs and get Ros. We need to get moving." She gratefully left the room, and ran up the stairs, headed towards Ros' room. The door was locked. "Ros? It's me. Let's go, hon."

Her head hung lethargically between her legs as she waited for the nausea to pass. A low groan sauntered through her lips, as a throbbing ran up the side of her face like hot waves running along the edge of the shore. The bleeding from her lip had stopped, but the pain was still immense. Sequoia's voice echoed in her head sweetly, an angel calling out to her.

She tottered towards the door, and began to unlock it. The latch clicked loudly and the door screamed as Ros pulled it back. Ros stared at Sequoia with crimson, stormy grey eyes that were slightly puffed from crying. Black eyeliner or mascara scarred her cheeks, running into her mouth and down her chin. Her lips quivered. A clot of blood was forming darkly.

Sequoia's anger began to seethe. Her heart raced violently as she reached out and pulled her broken friend into her chest. Stroking her hair and madly apologizing, Sequoia began to weep. Her tears fell into Ros' black curls, drowning themselves in her hair.

The waves of nausea began to quiet down. The warmth from Sequoia's breath fell on her like a hundred sunlit kisses. The inaudible, crunchy whisper of her friend's apologies rolled around in her head slowly and sweetly, a jarful of honey spilling out of the bottle. She wanted all the rest of the world to fade and the only thing to remain was to be Sequoia's arms to hold her and keep her safe. So safe and warm and...

Breaking free from Sequoia was hard, but Ros needed to leave the den of evil, as she would lovingly call it. Sauntering into the bathroom, she stared at herself in the mirror. A horrid, drunk looked back. Only problem was she wasn't drunk, and she was angry at herself because she wasn't. "But that will soon change," she promised herself.

A stabbing fear and anxiousness began to swell within her chest. She turned on the faucet and went on to the laborious, but familiar task of cleaning up her mother's mess. Sequoia looked on as her friend scrubbed her bruised face. It gave her an eerie feeling that Ros was trying to scrub away the hurt within, and not the dirt without. Once she was all cleaned up, Ros whipped around and faced Sequoia with a wide smile. Her eyes glistened with tears to come, yet they never came. Her smile dropped to the floor like a hundred pound weight and revealed her thin, wan face. She began to tremble.

"What would I do without you?" Ros cried. Sequoia shook her head unbelievingly. Chills walked slowly through her body as Ros' voice penetrated and bounced around in her painful head. It was absurd. She felt absurd. Standing here with a secret searing in her chest and not being able to tell her. Not tell her now, cause she was breaking apart and besides that she, herself, was a coward. Sequoia tripped over to Ros' side and wrapped her arms around her. *Would she let me do this if she knew? Would she still love me if I told her that...?* The urgency to tell her washed away with Ros' breath as they hugged for what seemed infinity.

They bounded down the stairs ten minutes later in an obscenely normal way. As if nothing had happened at all.

"Bye father. Bye mother," Ros carefully said. Sequoia waved a meek goodbye as she walked out the door. The slam of the door pounded through the house as they left and mimicked Ros' mother's headache.

Ros' mother went to the kitchen to find her medicine. The splitting headache roared through her head, a '57 Chevy revving at the starting line in a drag race. She filled a glass of water. As she tried to twist off the cap of the prescription bottle, she knocked the glass over into the sink, shattering it. Heat began to form in the back of her eyes as she picked up the shards of glass. She picked them up harshly, piercing her calloused, dishwater hands. Hot tears streamed down her face in big, fat drops as she cleaned up her mess.

Her vision was blurred by the incessant running of tears. The chinking of shattered glass multiplied in her head one hundred times. Louder each time. 'No', she thought, '*I won't lose it again. No, she was behaving poorly. No, I am her mother and she is my daughter. No, I will not let you inside again. No, I did not hurt her. No, I won't hurt myself. No, I won't hurt myself. No, I won't hurt myself. No, I won't...*' she repeated in her head. Repeated it with each piece of broken glass. Repeated it till she didn't even realize she was saying it automatically. Then it started.

'*She lost her temper,*' a faraway voice chimed, '*bad Carlie! She is your flesh and blood.*' The sweet voice faded. Ros' mother dropped the pieces of glass back into the sink and began to shake convulsively.

'*No, I won't let you inside.*' she thought.

'*You worthless piece of...*' an angrier voice echoed, '*I can do what I want! Do it! Be with me! Do it!*' the voice screamed. The pitch of it's voice rose to the level of feedback on a guitar.

"No, I won't hurt myself! No, I won't hurt myself. No, I won't..." she wailed loudly. Ros' mother fell clumsily to her knees and began to sob hysterically. The voice kept calling out to her, calling her name in that same gruff, evil manner. Then slowly it died away.

'*She's your daughter.*' the sweeter voice returned, '*To take care of not to hurt. To love, not to hate. You should be ashamed!*' it sang. The sweeter voice rippled in her head, saying and singing, '*You should be ashamed!*'

"I'm sorry! I'm so sorry. I'm so sorry..." she screeched. It rang horrifyingly through the house.

The man with the small ferret eyes was in the living room, quiet and unsure. He took off his glasses, and pinched the bridge of his nose. He felt frightfully helpless; his wife was going crazy. He had heard all of her moaning and wailing and screaming. But he couldn't do anything. Just like when he saw her twist Ros' arm grotesquely when she was only eight. Just like when he saw her yank thick bundles of Ros' hair when she fifteen. Just like when he saw her punch his daughter full force in the face today. Watching the blood rip out of the confines of Ros' lips, watching the anger electrify out of his wife's fist, watching the tears jump out of his daughter's eyes. That was all he could do. Watch. Watch and... so, he did the only other thing he could do, now. He began to cry.

Once in the car, Ros buried her face into her hands and began to cry hysterically. An acrid feeling overflowed within Sequoia leaving her sour with anger. Only if she hadn't been late. She felt powerless and incapable of comforting Ros. She had always felt that way.

An excerpt from

lint

by Susan Ckuj

Absently, he jammed one of his thick hands between the cushions and the back of the couch. He felt something cool and metallic brush against his calloused fingertips. He closed his fist around whatever it was that was down there, and withdrew it like the metal claw of those arcade skill machines. Instead of a plastic digital watch, or a stuffed Tazmanian Devil sporting a do rag and a red leather vest, there sat, among a great deal of lint, a grimy silver coin. Upon closer inspection, he realized it was a nickel from 1974. He tossed it into the air a few times, catching it in his mouth. He winced at the taste, which was not unlike that of aluminum foil. He peered at it closely, noting every detail. He hadn't ever noticed the minuscule letter `D' immediately to the left of...well,.whoever it was whose portrait graced the front of a nickel. He laughed to himself at the guy's hairdo. It reminded him of all the party fro's sported by guys with whom he used to work. You know the party fro...that haircut most often seen on guys who hang out at the Thirsty Whale. Short and spiky on top, shaved on the sides, a little longer in back until the nape of the neck, at which point long hair magically appears and cascades down the back in flowing golden spirals.

He was busying himself with the earthly question of whether or not the guy on the front of the nickel had owned a sparkly blue Trans Am and an extensive collection of Great White cassettes, when there was a knock on the door. He rose slowly, as the person on the other side of the door continued his incessant pounding. He swigged his beer, and ambled sluggishly to the door. He peered curiously through the glass eyehole. He saw nothing—apparently, the person on the other side of the door had commenced to putting his finger over the hole, obscuring his identity. What were the odds that it was a mass murderer? Was he hoping? He put his hand to the knob, nudged his hip into the door as he turned, and pulled...

Low Self Esteem

by Angela Bell

It was a lovely sunny morning. In classroom #206, Mrs. Ingwotho, the eighth grade teacher of Southbend Elementary School, was giving her students their homework assignment.

"Class, your assignment for today is to describe yourself in two words. Then, explain why those words best describe you. This is the only homework I'm giving tonight, because I want you to really concentrate on this assignment. Class, put your heart into this assignment. I'm curious as to what you individually think about yourselves. Also, because I want you to answer truthfully, I promise to keep all names confidential. OK? Class dismissed."

Audrey, one of the students in Room 206, was seriously thinking of her assignment for the night. But, no matter how hard she thought, the only words she could come up with were "worthless failure". Why would she describe herself in those two particular words? When did she start to feel this way about herself?

It all started back in 6th grade, around the time her parents divorced. Audrey did her best to try to keep them together, but she failed and they divorced, despite her efforts. She started to feel she couldn't do anything right.

Then, by the middle of sixth grade, Audrey knew she was a failure. The days of her mom starting to date had come! Audrey just couldn't understand why her mom even wanted to date, so she decided to ask her. Audrey will never forget what her mom told her.

"Mom, why do you date all the time? Why do you have to date at all?"

"Oh, Audrey," her mom said, "I'm not happy with my life or with who I am. You see, dating makes me feel younger, happier and good about myself. I wasn't happy before. Do you understand, Audrey?"

"Yes, I understand." she replied.

But silently she thought, "...yea, I understand perfectly. I don't make you happy enough, so you need someone else. I make you feel old, unhappy and bad about yourself because I remind you of daddy." Audrey wouldn't dare tell her mom what she was thinking because she would only deny it. But, Audrey knew that was what she was trying to say.

Now, in the seventh grade, Audrey was still trying her best, but no matter how hard she tried, she couldn't make her mother happy. Despite her hard work, she would always end up with D's and F's. It made her mother very upset.

"I know you can do better. Why don't you just try harder?," her mother asked, as she left for work that night. She had been working the night shift ever since she had met and married Chris.

So, Audrey was left with her stepfather.

"I think you do this on purpose to aggravate your mom." said Chris. "These are worthless grades. You can't get into any college with these grades. You can't graduate from elementary school, let alone high school. Audrey, if you don't change you're going to grow up to be a WORTHLESS FAILURE. Is that what you want to become?"

Audrey didn't tell Chris she already knew she was a worthless failure. She couldn't do anything right in the first place. She had failed to keep her original family together. She failed to keep her mom happy. She couldn't even keep her grades up so her mom wouldn't be upset, or so she could do something with her life. She was pitiful.

Audrey was now, in the eighth grade. Even though her grades had improved a little from where they were last year, Audrey still felt the same way about herself. With the assignment she had been given by her teacher, she knew what she would write.. "Maybe Mrs. Ingwotho would understand and know her for the worthless person that she was." With that in mind, she began her assignment.

"WORTHLESS FAILURE"
by Audrey Stoner

These words best describe me because it's who I am and all I'll ever be. I can't do anything right. Because of ME, my family fell apart. Because of ME my mom is unhappy. I'm not even capable of doing anything right for myself. I know no other words could describe me better. I'm too pitiful for any other words.

After reading the assignment, Mrs. Ingwotho asked Audrey to see her after school. Audrey automatically assumed she had done something wrong. She was known for that.

"Audrey, I especially wanted to talk to you because your assignment touched my heart. Now I know that I'm only your teacher and that my opinion is my opinion, and you may think it doesn't really count. I believe you're among the top students here. I'm aware of your grades last year and how low they were. But, I'm also aware of how you've been working extra hard this year, and gradually they're getting better. I know that compliments about personal abilities don't mean a think if that person doesn't believe in them, so, I'm not going to just keep telling you. I'm going to try and help you. Here's the deal. If you'll consent to changing your two word assignment to 'Low Self-Esteem', I'll not only give you an A+, but I'll also become your friend and do my best to help you improve your confidence. We'll do it together, ok, Audrey?"

"Ok, Mrs. Ingwotho."

After the talk, with Mrs. Ingwotho, Audrey began to feel better about herself. Mrs. Ingwotho spent time with her every day, just as she had promised. Audrey's grades soared. Even after she left Mrs. Ingwotho's room, the confidence and friendship Mrs. Ingwotho brought into her life helped Audrey all the way through her last year in grammar school and all through her high school.

An excerpt from

Love Hurts

by Shimika Parker

Hopelessness

After the last tragic moment with the rapist, I immediately called the cops to have Marc cuffed. I didn't know what good it would do. I felt dirty and rotten. I yearned to die; my instincts advised me not to. I was a dead soul with a moving body. I was living in hopelessness and depression. Hot flames of fireballs formed deep in my soul. My heart contained hot lava waiting to erupt. I despised the person who took away my innocence. Every moment of my life was like a bomb ticking, ready to explode.

After Marc destroyed me, my life changed drastically. My emotions were like the weather. One minute I was quiet and somber, the next I was insane. My screams rang out into the night. The tears on my anguished face, wet and burning, kept on falling down like the raindrops on my windowpane.

I didn't know how I would survive. Nothing tasted sweet. Candy tasted bitter. Just when I thought my life had enough bitterness in the melting pot of torture, I was told by the doctor that I was three months pregnant. There was an aching pain inside my heart. It was burning. The burning of acid. The kind that wouldn't let you die peacefully, and won't let you live happily.

I never believed in killing an innocent child. My thoughts were to bring it into the world and have another family to raise it. I didn't have the ability to mother a child. It was cruel, but what was I to do? I was still a baby. My main priority was to graduate from college and become successful.

When I am ready to handle the pressure, I'll take her back. If I raise her, I'm bound to abuse her. I don't want to follow in my parents' footsteps. I don't want to hurt anyone. I don't want her to feel what I felt. She shouldn't be anguished or isolated. I don't want her to feel unwanted. I need her very much. As much as it killed me, I putted her up for adoption. I knew it was going to affect us both, but that was the only possible option available.

After losing my precious one, I lived life deaf and blind. Life became pure hell. I was digging a grave for myself. I locked myself in my room, isolated from the world. I blamed myself for what happened. I felt down and I constantly cried myself to sleep. The sound of tear drops was like a lullaby. Most of the time it was a challenge to even close my eyes at all. The vision of my baby reaching out her innocent, infant arms, crying for her mother's embrace kept haunting me.

I felt wicked. I wanted to go to the police and confess the crime that I committed. I should've been locked up for abandoning my child. I shouldn't have neglected Christy.

The guilt had taken me over. I abused myself in many ways, not realizing I was imitating my parents. I would take a knife and slit my wrist to see the blood pour. I'd cry and then I'd laugh. I was going nuts. I starved myself for days. My roommates forced me to eat. They shoved food into my mouth when I was intolerant. They were only doing it for my own good. I hadn't noticed their sincerity, because I felt everyone out there was against me. Now I realize they are my two best friends. No, they are more than that, they are my sisters. My family.

My roommates saw the situation I had to face, and they suggested I get professional help. I didn't listen to them at first. They told me if I continued to act this way, I could possibly die. I was happy deep down to hear my future told. They made me understand I must live for my baby. I set up an appointment with Dr. Kramer, a therapist. She sat down with me and paid attention to what I said. She wasn't like other people, she was interested in what I had to say (well, she was paid to listen to people). I was confident in telling her my inner emotions. I recalled the moment I was abused by my "role models". I felt really uncomfortable when I told her about my wildest fantasy, to die happy. I confided in her and told her why I thought about dying. I reminisced about the times I felt happy and loved. I told her how much being a part of someone's life meant to me. She understood me when I told her I wanted to feel special.

I felt relieved after telling her my story. I asked if I could be helped. She said, "Yes, if I believed in myself." I've never believed in my actions. Everything I did was wrong. No one has ever believed in me before, but she was an exception. She helped me gain self-confidence and self-respect. After our confidential talks, I began to eat more. The food tasted sweeter and the air smelled fresh again.

On my final session with Dr. Kramer, she advised me to keep a journal of my daily life. She suggested I put my every thought and feeling into this diary to make me feel better. She was right. I feel like a whole new person. To me, writing this diary is a way of releasing my soul into a whole new world. Dr. Kramer told me that if I buried my feelings deep inside I could possibly turn into a bitter old grump like before. Therefore, everything that I have never told anyone (except Dr. Kramer) has been confided in this journal.

Starting Over

My baby has finally come home. I know I said I was going to wait until I graduated college before I have custody of Christy, but I missed her very much. She'll turn two years old this coming Wednesday. I go to work in the morning waiting tables, and at night I attend college. I am struggling to put food on the table, but that's okay. As long as I can be with my baby, I can sacrifice. I have one more year to go before I receive my bachelor's degree in computer programming. I am pretty fortunate to have friends who would babysit Christy without cost.

Lucy is a true friend. She was one of my roommates. She plays with Christy and teaches her new things. Christy is really fond of Lucy. I am glad Lucy takes pleasure in babysitting for me. Even though she insists on not taking my money, I felt I needed to repay her in some way. I take her to the movies or to dinner at times. I guess that was the only way I knew how to show her my gratitude.

Even though my perspective on life has changed, sometimes I feel depressed. I feel like I didn't do a good job of raising Christy. I constantly blame myself. I live in guilt, but then I look at the bright side of things and say, "at least I tried my best." I would never think of killing myself, because Christy depends on me to survive. I grit my teeth and scream, letting out all my anger and frustration.

Christy is a disobedient child. She doesn't listen to a word I say. She is a very hard child to raise, but I will try my very best. It's hard sometimes not to give her a spanking, however, I would never think of misusing my authority. I love her more than life itself. She will receive all the love that I never received. She will grow up in a normal home, and live a normal life. She will have friends, hopes and dreams, and a bright future ahead of her.

An excerpt from

No Time for Tears
by Ivy Jackson

"Mother, you have to get up before daddy comes in and finds you like this," pleaded Sabrina.

Joi's head was cloudy, but she was conscious.

"I'm fine, Sabrina. I thought you said your father molested you. I must have been mistaken," smiled Joi as she rose to her feet.

"He did," whispered Sabrina.

Joi wavered, but did she didn't pass out.

"Who put such a stupid idea in your head," questioned Joi.

"No one did, I remember everything."

"What exactly do you remember?," asked Joi.

"I already told you. Please don't make me say it again," cried Sabrina.

"Just fill me in on the basics," responded Joi.

"It started when I was six and ended when I was eleven. He made me do all kinds of gross things. He even had some videotapes."

"Where was I while all of this was going on," questioned Joi.

"You were always away on more important business," replied Sabrina.

"Are you trying to imply that I am responsible for what happened to you?"

"Of course not, mother. No one's to blame except daddy."

Joi sat down on the bed and stared off into space, "I can't believe

Walter would do those things. He loves you too much."

"Mother, I remember something else!"

"What is it?"

"Daddy took pictures of the two of us together."

"That's nothing new. The two of you have tons of pictures together."

"These aren't average looking pictures," replied Sabrina.

"I'm sure he's destroyed them by now," said Joi.

"No, I remember the last time I was here he was staring at pictures. He hid them in his desk drawer. You have to go get them."

"Why can't you go," mumbled Joi.

"Because I'm not prepared to see daddy. Please go, mother. This will be the proof you need to believe me."

Joi left the room swiftly. Sabrina grabbed the covers off the bed and wrapped them tightly around her. She had a chill, but it wasn't something heat could cure. The emptiness she'd felt earlier was still there, but it was slowly being filled with anger and disgust.

Joi came back into the room, her face was pale and her hands were shaking. Sabrina snatched the photos from her and the moan that escaped her lips was one of disgust.

All the pictures were of Sabrina at various stages during the molestation. She was naked in each picture, but she wasn't alone. In some of them Sabrina was performing sexual acts on her father and in others she was doing things to herself.

Sabrina turned around once she realized Joi was crying.

"I can't believe that bastard did those things to you," sobbed Joi.

Sabrina was at a loss for words. She couldn't believe her father had done it either. She knew what he had done, but the pictures made it more of a reality. What had made an almost perfect man commit an act of violence against his daughter? Sabrina wanted to know the answer to that.

"What are you going to do now," questioned Joi.

"I won't let this control my life. I will get through this," Sabrina said, as she looked at her mother. "We'll get through it together."

"Sabrina, I've never been there for you in the past. What can I do to make your future better?"

"Come with me, mother. We'll go to my job in the Bahamas. That will give us a chance to decide what to do next. We'll make a whole new life for ourselves."

Joi shook her head. "I can't do that, Sabrina. I love you, but I can't go away."

"Why not," asked Sabrina.

"I haven't had the best life, Sabrina, I was born dirt poor. My father left the day I was born and my mother was a housekeeper. I made a vow to myself that I wouldn't become like either of them. I wanted to become rich and famous."

"What does that have to do with coming with me?"

"When I was a teenager, I was out of control. I left home when I was sixteen and I hung around with men I thought could give me something. I was very beautiful, in fact, you're my spitting image. I realized the men were only after getting their own needs met, so I forgot about being rich and famous, I just wanted to be loved. When I met Walter, I convinced him and myself that I loved him. After a year, I realized I hated Walter, but loved the money. I decided to have the best of both worlds. I used Walter for the money and I had younger men for the temporary love. Your father knew about these men, but he didn't seem to care. In the end I was rich and miserable," sighed Joi.

"Mother, you don't have to be miserable. If you come with me, I promise you won't be. I have enough money to take care of the both of us," replied Sabrina.

Joi shook her head again, "That's your own personal money. You've done something I could never do. You've made a life for yourself. I'm proud of you. I may not always show it, but I really admire and respect you. That's why you have to go and make a life for yourself . I'll stay here."

"How can you stay with a man you know molested your daughter?," asked Sabrina.

"It'll be difficult, but I have to."

"Why do I feel like you're choosing money over me?"

Joi just looked away.

"I love you Sabrina."

Sabrina was a little hurt, but she accepted that as an answer. They hugged each other and at that moment, Walter walked in.

"Sabrina, why didn't you tell me you were here?"

Joi let go of Sabrina and stormed over to Walter.

"You stay away from her, you disgusting, perverted, bastard."

"What's your problem," Walter asked. "Sabrina, come give me a hug."

Sabrina began to cry again, "I don't know what you did, daddy. How could you?"

"What are you talking about? Joi, what have you put in her head?"

"I didn't put anything in her head."

Joi searched for the pictures.

"Do these look familiar?"

Walter stared at the pictures then at Sabrina.

"Sabrina, I can explain these."

"You don't have to. I remember everything. All along you had me convinced that mother didn't love me. All the while it was you with your twisted, warped out, perverted brain. Why did you do it, daddy," sobbed Sabrina.

"Let me explain," pleaded Walter, "It was all Joi's fault. She neglected me and I didn't have anywhere else to turn."

"How dare you blame this on me, Walter. I'm not the sicko that molested my own daughter," spat Joi.

Walter ignored Joi, " I did it because I love you. Those moments we had together were done through love. You enjoyed it too because you never told anyone."

"You're crazier than I thought. The reason I never told anyone was because you brainwashed me into believing that you loved me. I was a child. What kind of pleasure could I get from a grown man. No, a better question is what kind of pleasure could a grown man get from a child?"

"Sabrina, you really don't understand. I'm not the enemy, Joi is."

"There is no one to blame but yourself. I loved you and you used that against me. You knew I would have done anything you asked me."

"Sabrina, listen to me. You're mother has you confused. I'm not the bad one here, she is. She deserted us when we needed her the most. We had to comfort each other, it was mutual. Don't you remember that?," Walter pleaded.

"Daddy, I'm not the naive little girl you molested. Those mind games you play don't work on me anymore. You didn't do it because you loved me. If you really loved me you would have kept your hands to yourself."

"Sabrina, I did love you and still do. You've taken things out of pro-portion," whined Walter.

"I'm amazed that I didn't know how sick you are. You really need help. I'm better off knowing what you really are. I can go on with my life, but you'll have to live with what you did to me for the rest of your life."

"Sabrina, try to understand."

"I won't let this pull me down. It's just a stumbling block that I have to step over. The good thing about remembering is that you can also forget and that's exactly what I'm going to do. I'm going to forget the molestation, the pain, the anger, the emptiness, but most importantly, I'm going to forget you. I don't need you because I have myself. I finally realized that was all I ever needed," cried Sabrina.

"Please, Sabrina, you have to understand," pleaded Walter.

Sabrina wiped the tears from her face and turned towards her mother.

"I don't want to leave you, but since you choose to stay, that's your business. You know where I can be reached."

Sabrina walked out of the room and out of her parents life.

Statues of Jesus

by Lauren Mizock

Phoebe felt God had made it so that George had AIDS, that it was his destiny, that he was born to die, as was his father. He remembered how his father had withered away at the end, like a flower. After chemotherapy, he was almost invisible among all those rose-colored, linen sheets. There was a slight movement in his chest, and his body would rise and fall, like the smoke of a volcano soon to be extinguished. And George would just hide behind the doorway a little and watch his father existing, yet fading like a sunset, where the sun drooped down those rose-colored sheets.

George panicked at the thought of his own withering, brought about by the black spots of Kaposi's Sarcoma he started finding on his cheeks and arms months ago. He grew a beard and wore only long-sleeved shirts after that. George used to be a model, disarming, personable. This destruction of his vanity troubled him, and he'd remind himself of how he wasn't the same person as he was before, when he met David.

★★★★★

He was at the gay night-club he went to every Saturday night and spotted David across the floor, dancing under the strobe lights. The greens and reds clung to his shiny skin. David found himself being checked out and walked over. George bought him a drink.

"I've never seen you here before."
"I've seen you."
Sentences spilled from their mouths, flirtations, the language of lovers. George watched beads of sweat run down David's chest under a tight tank top. His smooth, sleek skin was vibrant under the disco lights. They went back to George's apartment. It was a short night, and he never saw David again. Their relationship had risen and fallen like the outline of David's face in the shade of George's bedroom. He was lying in bed, the sheets draped across half of his naked body like one of those statues of Jesus, George thought to himself, when David sat up, put his shoes on, and slipped his shirt over his black, feathery head of hair.
"Bye."

"Bye." George smiled at David before he walked out of the room. He listened for the sound of the door locking in place and then turned over and stared at the light pouring in through the cracks of his iron blinds.

George wished he had resisted his blue eyes, his smile. He wished he'd been more cautious with his blood.

★★★★★★

"George, honey, you're falling asleep. I'll help you into bed." She grabbed hold of his elbow and escorted him into his room again.

"Say your prayers and go to sleep." His muscles ached and throbbed worse than ever. He looked up at his mother, lying prostrate at his side. Squinting, her head illuminated in the sunlight, white, wispy hair floating lifelessly around her like a halo. He couldn't tell if she was the mother from his youth, or from the future, after her death. The image of her looking like an angel displaced him.

She walked out of the room, with steps almost as cautious and tired as his own. He thought, lying in bed, more exhausted than ever before, "This is it. I'm gonna die in my sleep like my father. I'm gonna die like that butthead who was addicted to his painkillers. I'm gonna fall asleep like him, and never wake up." The sleepiness dragged him away from those thoughts.

"Welcome." A hollow voice reverberated like low-pitched wind chimes. George was surrounded by people who looked like the sunny image he was left with his mother. They seemed to float atop a smokey ground...but purer than any night club gas, it was that of clouds...of the heavens. He felt like he'd risen so high in the sky that it was barely blue anymore. The air was calm. George felt weight-less...without a body to make move, drag slowly from place to place, trying not to hurt. And that sadness wasn't inside of him anymore. The lingering hopelessness constantly caught in his throat was gone. What was left in its place was numbness. Fear was an emotion banned from this place, but if he could, he would fear the sensation that control over his mind was about to be vacuumed out of his head. George held onto his thoughts.

He heard the voice again. "Congratulations. You have been chosen for Heaven."

He looked up to whatever sky was left above him to locate the being behind the voice.

"Your guardian angel will show you around." David stood before him, in wings and white robe, lit by sunlight.

"Hi, George. Good to see you again."

"David. You look...good." David's face went grave. "George. I'm sorry."

"I know."

Let me show you around," David glided towards a fountain. "Imported Venetian glasses, fountains containing endless supplies of Dom Perignon."

They came to a platform of people lit up by spotlights and a disco ball. A dance club, laying disco, house, or whatever you fancy. I know you loved the night life. They know what you like up here too, and they'll get it for you."

"What if I just want to talk to you?"

"Shoot." David waited.

"How've you been?"

"I've been okay. Everything's fine."

"Are you seeing anybody?" George imagined David would say something flirty like, "I've been seeing you," joking about being his guardian angel.

"Things aren't like that up here. You don't need relationships like that. You get the feeling that everyone is yours and their own. It's not the same as being down there."

"Well, I'm the same."

"You just got here." *No Honey, no Georgie. David doesn't even flail his arms a bit like he used to, making fun of himself.*

"What if I don't want to change? What if I want to stay the same. What if I never believed in 'God' or Heaven anyway?" It was hard for George to get angry because it was a feeling trying to be sucked out of his head.

"George. Please."

"You're not even David anymore. You've changed. You're not like I knew you." David disappeared, looking like a mild version of a Jesus statue. An office-like room materialized around him along with a brown leather swivel desk chair, hanging plants, a window overlooking a pond and a valley, and bookshelves lined with Freud, Darwin, the Bible, Shakespeare, and Danielle Steele. A statue of a crucified Jesus hung over the bookcase. George noticed something about the face he'd never noticed before, an expression of tranquility. Like on the faces of Buddhas and the look his mother gets when she prays, her body still, kneeling beside the bed. George thought that maybe religion was more of a form of spirituality for her, like monks...a means of meditation.

"George," a tall-looking white man with a gray beard appeared in the chair, "what seems to be the problem?" He turned a little in the chair, held a pen between his hands, and eyed George patiently.

"What do you think?"

"A bit of a cliche aren't we? But, I didn't believe in you, anyway."

"I think you should re-evaluate that idea."

"How can I get out of here? Can you commit suicide in Heaven?"

"You don't want to take it downstairs, do you?"

"There's a Hell too?"

God was silent a moment. "This is the way you always thought things would be."

"No, I thought there'd be blackness, rest. Not a dampening on my real feelings to produce some sick form of happiness."

"Your truth, your reality."

George glanced at the Freud section of God's library. "So, what you're saying is that my subconscious wish was for happiness after death, an end to suffering."

"What do you think?"

"Jesus, you're sounding like my shrink!"

God clicked his tongue. "We don't say his name in vain." His mother used to always say that.

"I don't feel anything here. Without sadness and hurt, happiness doesn't feel real. It feels more numbing." George wasn't about to fall into his subconscious ideal world. George felt a strong feeling in him once again before God stroked his beard in thought, and the room became transparent, then faded away. For a minute, he was about to try to find the secretary to set up another appointment out of habit with his own psychiatrist. George walked through the clouds this time instead of on top of them, signifying his renewed mortality. He had the sense that he was choosing his environment, his lifestyle. George felt now that he had control over his own reality by believing in it.

He fell to Earth with his eyes closed, being able to see the land coming closer without needing to use his eyesight. And maybe none of it was truly happening anyway, maybe he was never really in Heaven in the first place.

George fell into his body comfortably, accepting the aching in his side, the pain in his legs. He rolled over and opened his eyes, yawned, and looked into the sun, bleaching his body along the crusty rug.

★★★★★★

Phoebe entered the room. "Did you sleep okay?"

"Yeah."

Phoebe became distracted by the window. "Oh, the light is right in your eyes. Let me close the shades."

"No, Mom. Leave it. The sun feels good today."

Water for a Bridge

by Colin Harris

Even the fluff of dandelions seemed to know what was wrong. It was one of those days seemingly made for dandelions, when they all shed their seeds, the stem left bare, and the seeds fly out west, to settle down in a lush prairie somewhere near the edge of the world. Or east maybe, to play in the cool coast breezes, only to arrive in Father Donnely's garden, a pious man who'd never infringe upon the right of a weed to grow right there in his tulips. But it was all wrong, and the dandelion seeds circled the Earth cautiously, finally settling in the sun-baked soil, somehow realizing that this was the end for them. No drought, there was sufficient water for drinking, and the trees were all alive. But the heat!

Such heat the town had never seen! It settled in the trees, it swam the murky waters, but most importantly, it dug it's scorching talons into the hearts of the population. The children, too tired to play, found new and inventive ways to trouble their mothers. The men, exhausted from a fruitless days labor, stalked into their houses without a word of greeting, and sat in their gilded armchairs, starting at their hands. The blazing inferno settled over the town long ago, a pall with one solitary purpose: to strangle the life from each and every innocent of this burg, and disappear without a trace, flitting away like a zephyr. The worst part of it was that nobody knew what was wrong. Everyone put the heat at the back of their minds along with the rest of their troubles and continued along with the usual routine, becoming more bitter and less human by the minute. Everyone, that is, except Ezra.

It seems like every small hamlet has an Ezra. Regardless of the century, hemisphere, background, or any other myriad variances in the known universe, there is always an Ezra. The kind of guy who lives on the edge of town, as opposed to the inside. The kind of man the town urchins furtively seek to catch a glimpse of, only to turn tail and run at the slightest crackling of an autumn leaf, mewling for their mothers. The kind of man lovingly referred to as "Crazy Ol (name)". That's how Ezra was thought of, and that was just fine with him. He kept mostly to himself, ponderin', congitatin', syncronizin', pontificatin', salivatin', ruminatin', but always relaxatin'. But, boy did he think! He sat and stared , stared so hard his eyes ached, and he thought about things.

That's probably why everybody dismissed him as crazy. He would always stare deep into a body's eyes whenever they said a word, and he was silent as a cathedral.

One day while he was quietly sitting and thinking, the evening sun sat lazily lolling on its hook in the great expanse of sky. Ezra looked up and said, "Its too damn hot out here!" And it had to be as hot as Tarterus for Ezra to have spoken a word, let alone a whole sentence. He looked at the pitifully cracked and dried river bed that flanked his house, and an idea came to him. It was an idea entirely out of the ordinary, and most folks would dismiss it as crazy, but that was Ezra for you. Being hot, it was perfectly logical and sound that he would begin to think about water. He thought of the Yangtze River, and how that sounded, and where had he heard that? He imagined himself a wave, a wave of immaculate cobalt blue, leaping toward her lunar majesty. He traversed the world, carried ships to their doom, seethed, foamed, died, and was reborn. He dreamed he was a typhoon, he grew in anger and ferocity and despoiled the coasts of a hundred countries, immolated kings and priests alike. A force of nature annihilating without prejudice. He thought of archaic hulks of blue-white ice, geysers blasting in a cacophony of seething aquatic elements, but his mind got a hold of himself, took a deep breath, and set itself back upon the more mundane topic of rivers. He darted in the waters like a glistening pike, and sat lazily in the sand like a fat catfish. He thought of boats, bait, boys, then bridges. Bridges were kind of strange, Ezra thought. They were always over water. In fact, he couldn't think of a single bridge that had been built that didn't have something under it. And then Ezra smiled his wrinkled smile, because he had his solution. He had thought out, in his own convoluted way, how to bring blessed relief from the abominable heat for himself, as well as those in the town who had shunned him all those years. Most "normal" folks, when confronted with a body of water of manageable size, would see the need for a bridge. Ezra, on the other hand worked in reverse. He was thinking, when confronted with a bridge of manageable size, somehow nature would see the need for a body of water. He would build the bridge, and the water would flow clear and cold, spawned from mountain streams and rivulets of melted snow.

How to go about building it was never a concern for him. He marched out, the sun glinting about his bald pate, a Spartan warrior adorned for the impending battle. The first thing was to procure stones for his momentous task. Luckily, a long-abandoned quarry skirted the town about twenty miles to the east. Ezra hitched up his wagon to Bella, an irascible old mare who had seen him through countless harvests, and set off onto the road, the sun transforming him and Bella into unfathomable stencils against its blinding majesty.

The quarry stood at the edge of the woods Ezra frequented as a child. The quarry was silent and foreboding, a giant pit thirty feet at its center. The concentric circles of rock served to create a makeshift Roman coliseum, with titanic hulks of rock jutting from the ground at random. Ezra strode toward the giant stone graveyard with purpose. He sat before a man-sized piece of granite like a sculptor, hammer and chisel in hand, and he began to nibble at the stone bit by bit until a large chunk hit the earth with a resounding CRACK! Even the rocks' stoic mass seemed to sag beneath the crushing weight of Ezra's unceasing toil. On and on, he chiseled the granite and shale until the sun sank below the trees, and the only sound was the lonely ring of Ezra's tools. Then, it stopped silently at his hands, knobby road maps of his life's choices. He looked at the rough stone he was hewing, saw its mottled surface. He looked at his hands, he looked at the stone, and he was confused. Maybe he was wrong. Maybe they were not right, and he was a simple old codger, a little touched in the head, and he should stop this nonsense at once and finally become a productive member of society. But just then, doubt perching on his shoulder like a slithering little imp, the clouds moved off the moon, and the lunar glow turned the rough stone to the most beautiful marble he had ever seen. The stars whirled above his head, the wind kicked up and blew dust in his eyes, and Ezra's laugh could be heard for miles. He had his answer.

He had realized long ago this would be the last thing he ever did.

Dorchester Commons

by Selly Thiam

The apartment building stuckout like a sore thumb compared to all the other apartment buildings on Dorchester. A big tan canopy hung over the entrance that read" Dorchester Commons" in fancy writing, but everybody called it "the Complex."

Daniel sat on the front steps watching a Sprite can roll past. He removed a pack of Camel's from his pocket. He lit a cigarette, took a long hard drag, and felt the smoke roll down his throat.

Someone new had moved in. He had seen him this morning. He knew that he had moved in with the "Two Disciples" that live on the third floor. Daniel smiled. The "Two Disciples" was the nickname given to the two gay men that lived in the building. "Mark and John," he thought to himself.

"How many times do I have to tell you that smoking kills brain cells!", a voice yelled from the door of the complex.

"It depends on what I'm smoking!", Daniel yelled back.

Anet walked out and sat down next to Daniel.

"How about you give me one of them Camels?"

"I thought smoking kills brain cells?" He handed her a cigarette and a book of matches.

"I thought you said it depends on what we're smoking."

Anet sat on the front steps and reached for Daniel's hand. She loved Daniel, not like a lover, but like a brother. Daniel had been there for her.

"What's wrong?" The question had slipped from Daniel's lips before he knew what he was going to ask.

"There's a baby growing inside of me,"she said very calmly. There was a long pause.

"Who's the father?"

"It's not important," Anet continued.

"Well, what are you going to do?"

"I don't know," she finished.

Daniel sat there not knowing how to respond. He knew that he was disappointed in Anet for doing this to herself. All those years they had spent together in school, Daniel knew that she wasn't stupid. But he didn't understand why she was so calm about the whole thing. Then he realized something. This was Anet. She never worried about anything. She never cared how the world perceived her. She was seventeen years old, but swore she knew everything. She would walk to the ends of the earth for anyone she loved, and if she had this baby, Daniel knew that she was going to be okay. He understood that this baby would be loved and hopefully would become a replica of it's mother. It made Daniel think about his own mother, someone he once wanted to be like.

"The boy who imagines that the world is against him has generally conspired to make it true."
"Never let the fear of striking out get in your way."

His mother, the women who lived in a world of quotes. The woman who taught him how school is important to success. The woman who he overheard at night screaming for her life as his father beat her. The woman who prayed and cried that Daniel would never become like his father, and that he would turn out to be better than her. Daniel always wondered if it was his fault that she stayed so long with her husband.

"It is important that a boy have two parents. It is important that you understand that no matter how much you think it is your fault that I'm still here, it is my decision. I have the power over my own destiny, just like you will always have the power over yours."

One night he heard his mother screaming. He heard his fathers fist slamming against his mother's face. Daniel got up and ran to her aid. There she lay, his mother, the most beautiful woman he knew, in the middle of the floor begging for her life. Daniel stared at his father. How could he do this to her? How could he terrorize her like this?

Why didn't he understand that she was special, that she was beautiful? Daniel's anger ran through him and he jumped at his father's throat. Daniel wanted to kill him. He wanted to make him feel how he made his mother feel every night. Daniel's father nearly killed him. He beat him like he was a stranger, like Daniel wasn't his son. The next morning his mother was gone, and on his dresser sat a note that had his name written on it in calligraphy.

"Daniel,
I'm sorry I've left you. I'm sorry I couldn't be the mother you needed me to be. I need to go. I can't stay here if I want to maintain my sanity. I'm sorry that I can't see you grow up. I'm sorry that I let you live in such a horrible environment. Just remember that the world is yours to play in. Remember that you create your own destiny. I will always love you and one day I will be back to see you again.

Love,
Mom"

The woman who lived in a world of quotes was gone. She had followed her own destiny and had left Daniel there to live out the remainder of his childhood years with his father. A man who had no idea what it felt like to be special. Daniel hated her after that day and he never saw her again.

"Daniel what are you thinking about? I hope your not thinking about me. You know I'll be fine." Anet held on to Daniel's hand a little tighter.

"Yea, I know."

Just then a slender woman walked to the front of the steps.

"Excuse me," she whispered as though she were talking to herself. Anet and Daniel barely heard her.

"Hello," Anet projected a smile in the woman's direction. The woman returned the smile and walked into the apartment building.

"God, she is beautiful," Anet let her thought escape her lips.

"Yeah, but she never leaves her apartment."

Margaret's Story

The door shut behind her as she entered her basement apartment. It was like putting the lid on a coffin or closing the entrance of a tomb. Margaret was dead. She died with her husband and child in a fiery car accident.

"Margaret you weren't in the car. There is nothing you can do about it," her mother pleaded for Margaret's return to the land of the living. "Please honey. Remember we all lost something that day, you a child and a husband, and me, a grandchild and a son in law. Please Margaret, come visit me. Get out of that apartment."

Margaret had done a good job of pushing everyone away. She was trapped in the world she created for herself.

"Time is like a playful kitten. She creeps up on you and drinks the day like a bowl of milk." Her husband's words. He was a poet.

"So beautiful, so perfect," she thought. And her daughter. "So young, so full of life. She never had a chance to grow up. She was just like her father, so beautiful, so smart. She might have been a poet, she might have been anything."

Margaret had this conversation with herself many times. She knew it wasn't healthy, but she wondered. She wondered what it might have been like if her husband and daughter might have lived. She found herself crying as she had done every night before.

"They are gone." It was as if she realized it for the first time. They had been gone for three years now, but she relived the pain of losing them every day. She screamed for their return. "But Margaret, honey, they're dead." Of course her mother was right, but Margaret didn't want to believe it,and so she cried, like she did every night, until there were no more tears left to shed.

An excerpt from

Becoming One

by Clare Myers

a screech pierced the darkness. the goddesses clung together, trying to burn themselves in the other's body. they cried out in pain, tears covering their faces.

the land was frozen over, the sky black, or empty. only at the horizon did there appear a hint of light and color, slowly dissolving into nothing. the sisters clung to each other for warmth, for strength, for anything, feeling their world closing in, feeling their breath being ripped away.

it was as if the world were collapsing, as if we were the only ones who could be saved. i looked out at her, tearing at the pain, letting her eyes pierce my skin. her hands felt like ice against my neck, trying to calm me, but only making it harder to bear. i tried to look inside of her, inside her eyes, inside her soul. all i could see was myself. we melted into one another as i leaned to kiss her lips, a warm halo calming us, taking us in. the world fell away.

we are a ball of fire floating through the blackness. our thoughts, our souls, emerge as one, and we are at peace.

the goddesses lie, facing away from each other, collapsed into themselves, knees to chin, arms tangled around their flesh, hair wrapped about bodies, begging for warmth. all is dark, all is still; they do not breathe.

a gentle wind begins to blow, lifting the hair and exposing the soft flesh underneath. at each edge of the emptiness a light sparks, and becomes steady, lifting the darkness, bleeding into the void. a fiery red swims in arcs across the sky, leaving trails of white and blue and gold, radiating warth, breathing life into the sisters.

ivory blinks, beholding the radiance that has taken over their world. she watches as her sister rises to her knees, breathing slow, lazy breaths with her eyes closed, worshipping the strength.

they stand, walking together with right hands outstretched. as their palms touch, a soft yellow light emanates from the connection, reaching to the sky. all was still. there was calm.

Breakfast Lament
by Cristina Ortiz

I awoke to hear the loud snoring next to me. I hadn't slept peacefully at all that night. Maybe just two hours of sleep, I think. But I don't know.

The sweet aroma of that cloudy August morning followed me. I was surprised when I stepped outside that morning. It wasn't hot and humid like it usually is every morning. It was cool and chilly. I felt cold and weak, so I stepped back inside.

I sat on the old, wooden brown chair, and shivered. My mind was somewhere far away, somewhere I've never been before. The cool air went in through the broken window, and sent more shivers up my body. I was trembling violently by now, and I didn't know what to do.

I stood up and slowly walked to the window to watch the sunrise. I felt hot, burning tears run down my small cheeks. I stood there, and didn't make a sound. The tears would just run down continuously. Like a machine.

The memories came back. I hadn't even known they would be there. The memories of last night were there.

After four long years of love. But it was never lust. After four long years of glances. And nothing more than that. Everyday, I would see him. To and from school. In the train. Until one day we were two sitting in a lonely train. And he sat next to me.

An excerpt from

The Highway Man

by Margaret McCloskey

The stairway was cold, empty, the silver chrome railings reflecting the fluorescent glow from the lights above. He stood in front of the door, leaning against the frame, grateful for just a moment of warmth. Outside, the wind howled and the snow drifts piled up high. He shook out his thin jacket, hoping desperately to shake out the cold. It was so warm here. Warm. He remembered that feeling. It was a feeling you got when you knew everything was okay, when you knew that no matter what happened, something would always be there to catch you when you fall. That people around you loved you and cared what happened to you. Now here he was, pushing a cart full of glass bottles and aluminum cans, seeking warmth in the empty stairwell of an old apartment complex.

They wouldn't mind if he stayed here just one night. One night. . . that's all. There were chairs stacked in the corner of the room, folding card chairs, covered by a dust blanket. He took the blanket from the chairs and wrapped his shivering body in it. One night, that's all. He curled up, his thumb in his mouth, struggling to gather all the warmth of his body. Just one night.

"Sonny! Sonny! Son-nee!" Charyl Freeman banged on the door of the apartment. "Sonny! I know you're in there. Open up!"

Sonny Adams tentatively went to the door. "Who's there?", he called. Who would be banging on his door at three a.m.? Probably a tenant. As landlord and maintenance man, Sonny should have been used to being called on for any job at any hour of the day or night. At 68, Sonny was the most loved member of what he referred to as his extended family, in other words, the tenants of his apartment building. The reason they loved him was because he knew almost all, if not everything, about each of the tenants in his buildings, and he covered for them. He knew Charyl had a new man over every week, but told her mother that she had no time for boyfriends. He knew that Leo hadn't had a real job in two years, but still had enough funds to live in the most expensive apartment in the whole complex. He knew that Susan Kindwood was getting married to a third husband, but told her fiancé she'd been married only once before. Sonny knew the birthdays of every child in the Harper family (and there were eight). He knew that Nathan Travis ran a successful company downtown but had always wanted to control his own line of restaurants. He knew that Jeremy Fischer's personal pastime was to hack into government databases and download information about whatever he felt like he wanted to know at the time.

Somehow, Sonny knew that this information kept him closer to his tenants than he'd ever been to anyone in his life. He knew these people like he knew himself, as though each one were a part of him. Nothing that they could do would ever surprise him. He could understand what they were thinking without needing them to say it aloud.

He hoped they felt the same way about him. Just as he knew that Jeremy wouldn't want most people to know that he could easily find out whether or not they had a police record, he'd told some of them the most private aspects of his life. Such as the fact that his wife of twenty-nine years died two winters ago of lung cancer.

He'd spent the better part of his twenties and thirties as a tap dancer on Broadway in a chorus line of Fred Astaire moves. He never wanted to give up dancing; he wanted to become famous, to dance and sing and choreograph like Gene Kelly or Fred Astaire. But when he met Emmie, she wanted to settle down and have kids, so his dream went short-lived. They had five children, three boys and two girls, all of whom were in their twenties and married with their own families. None of whom ever called. Sonny had always wanted to go back to dancing, but the years seemed to leak by, and he never did. Now it was too late, he was near seventy, gas lights were more modern than his abilities. So he bought this apartment building and adopted the tenants as his own family.

"Sonny! It's Charyl. We need to talk."

Sonny shuffled to the door, the cords of his robe dangling and dragging across the floor. "It's three in the morning," he called to Charyl, rubbing his eyes. He reached blindly for the door latch, his vision still blurred by sleep. "Can't we do this later?"

Charyl bounded into the room, flounced over to the couch and plopped herself down on the sofa. "I don't think so. I want to discuss this now. I want you to get rid of the man in the basement..." she paused, "tonight."

Sonny lowered himself into a chair, massaging his forehead with the tips of three fingers. "Charyl, please, can't this wait?"

"You've been saying that for almost a week. When are you going to do something real about it? I figured that if I came here in the middle of the night, I'd get your attention and maybe you'd understand that everyone living in this building wants him out of here, and soon." Charyl crossed her arms defiantly over her chest.

Sighing, Sonny realized that Charyl was not going to leave until she had made her point. "Why?" he asked, looking up. "Why is it so imperative that he not live downstairs? The area he uses no one up here ever needs. I can't remember that last time I was down there. If no one needs it, why shouldn't he be able to use it? At least until it's warmer."

"What about the stuff? He's got Abby Harper's blanket down there. He probably got it from the laundry room, which means that he has access to the whole building! This is a potentially dangerous situation, Sonny. Maybe he'll find his way up here and break into one of the apartments," Charyl continued, her eyes widening at the thought. "We don't know what he's planning down there."

"He did not get it from the laundry room," Sonny replied, sighing. "Ben and Abby gave me the blanket to cover the folding chairs down there. They were collecting dust, and I wanted to protect them. I doubt if that blanket has seen the inside of a laundry room in a year. It probably smells like an old sock. And he does not have access to anywhere else in the building. The doors all have locks. He uses only the basement under the stairs."

"Speaking of which, how did he even get inside? Aren't those doors supposed to be locked? He must have broken the lock to get inside. Maybe he has a crowbar hidden down there. He could attack any one of us, it's a lethal weapon!"

Sonny groaned. "Charyl, it's the middle of winter. The lock probably froze and broke off by itself. It's almost forty years old anyway. I haven't used that doorway in years. Besides, if he had broken it down, one of us would have heard him knocking around down there." Sonny stood up and walked to the doorway. "And right now, I'd like to get some sleep. Maybe you could arrange to have a meeting of everyone. Then we can all look at everyone's point of view and make a group decision about this. . . issue." Pulling open the door, Sonny motioned Charyl into the hallway.

Charyl flounced by, annoyed by the conversation. "You know, Mr. Adams, I think I will do just that." She stepped into the hallway and slammed the door behind her.

Sonny tried to go back to sleep, but found that he couldn't. The man had been staying in the basement for almost a week and a half, an Sonny knew that everyone was uncomfortable with his presence, even intimidated.

The thing about it was, he felt fond of the man. It was sort of a comforting factor, he didn't know why. The fact that a total stranger who was so dirty you couldn't tell what race he was, and was liable to attack anyone at anytime was not a nice thought, Sonny admitted. So, why was he so reluctant to throw out the filthy, smelly, and potentially dangerous man?

He didn't feel terrorized, that was the thing. He felt, somehow, that the man was harmless, just someone who had a bit of bad luck and needed a place to stay. He had no objections to the fact that the man chose this apartment to shelter himself from the elements. He knew the others felt differently. They were afraid to open their doors lest the homeless boogie-man might be standing there wielding a knife and a wicked grin. No one talked to Sonny anymore. No more friendly shouts from the elevator, no more waves from any of the usually cheerful Harper children. Sonny felt isolated, alone, ostracized within his own family. The more he stood up for what he believed in, the more the people he once considered family stepped away from him, pushing him out of their reach, and into a corner. A box with three sides, and the doorway barred by an obstacle he didn't want to contemplate hurdling.

Sonny shut his eyes. He knew he was going to have to seriously think about this situation. He knew he didn't want to have to force the man to leave the basement. Everyone deserves a place to stay. But he knew that the longer he made his opinions about this clear, the closer he pushed them into a corner, a corner where they were forced to think seriously about their values and what kind of environment they wanted themselves and their children to live in. Sonny knew that when he was raising kids, he certainly wouldn't have wanted them to have to step over a pile of dirty flesh when they went out the door each day. He knew that if he were in the same situation he was forcing many of his tenants into, he wouldn't think twice about moving out, no matter how close he was to the landlord. It was like an endless circle, and either way, Sonny knew he was going to lose. He would lose the tenants, his family, the people he'd cared for more deeply than anything else during the years he'd owned this building. He was part of their lives; they knew his habits; he could recite theirs by heart. And he knew that despite how close he had been to the tenants, each one would find a new apartment in the blink of an eye, move out, and never look back, if Sonny didn't do as he was told.

Funny how that phrase seemed to haunt him. He could remember his father leaning over him when he'd done something wrong, his large right fist squeezing Sonny's left upper arm until it bruised, his sour breath hissing though his crooked and yellowing teeth, "Do as you're told." He could remember Emmie looking sweetly up into his face, pleading with her eyes for him to give up everything he'd ever wanted to do in his life, so she could have kids, suggesting with her attitude that whatever she wanted, she was going to get. He could remember being told "No" every time he stood up for something he thought was right. He wanted something different than what everyone else did. He said something other than what everyone else wanted to hear. Every time he spoke out for himself, he was yelled at, chastised, frowned upon, told to do what he was told.

Not this time. Sonny sat up. He'd had enough. How many times had he been asked to do what everyone else wanted, to change his opinion just this once, if he did it this way, everyone else would be happy.

No, there had to be a middle ground here. Maybe he could appeal to their hearts. He knew that somewhere, deep inside each of his beloved tenants, there was a soft spot for something. He'd just have to get each spot to shine through stronger than the thick shell each one had put on to protect themselves from whatever they were afraid they might feel if they looked too closely at the homeless man who was spending time in their basement staircase.

Eternal Journey
by Kevin Irmiter

"Excuse me, are you Ralph Heaton?"

"Huh?" Ralph looked up to see who had just addressed him. A fairly tall and distinguished-looking fellow with dark hair stood before him. He seemed refined and intelligent, yet at the same time very warm, open and friendly. Ralph decided he liked him.

"You are Ralph Heaton, correct?" He spoke with a very faint French accent, although his fluency in the English language was apparent.

"Yeah, that's me. Are you my guide?"

"Why, yes. My name is Camus. Albert Camus. I do not suppose you have ever heard of me?"

"Uhhh...no sorry. You in the movies or something?"

"No, I'm a writer, actually. You have never heard of The Stranger? The Plague?"

"Sorry, no I don't read much, mister."

"Existentialism?"

"Exis-what?"

"Never mind. I should have expected this, I suppose. They have a very ironic sense of humor down here. The Existentialist philosophy majors usually get stuck with Micky Mantle or something.'

"Micky Mantle? I love that guy! Do you know him? Man, he was my hero back when I—?"

"Yes, yes, as interesting as all of that sounds, we do have business to attend to, you know. Now, you are perfectly clear, I trust, on the fact that you have been sentenced to eternal damnation? I mean, you realize that there is no hope of getting out?"

"Oh sure. I mean, I always figured I'd end up down here, if there was such a place. I mean, I sure wouldn't expect to be up there with G-G-G-..."

"Oh, didn't anyone tell you? You can't say the G-word while you're down here."

"What about H-H-H-..."

"Oh you can say heaven. Just don't capitalize it."

"...heaven. Gotcha, thanks."

"In any case, it is good that you have accepted your fate. It will make things easier for you, trust me. So often people come down here absolutely convinced that they have don't nothing wrong and that they are victims of some cosmic mistake. This only makes things even more, er, hellish than they already are, no pun intended. Now then, my job is to take you to Minos. No rush, though... eternity is an awfully long time, and down here it doesn't matter much how long things take, as long as they get done eventually. Really, we have time to talk about anything, so don't be afraid to ask me any questions you may have on your mind."

"Who's Minos?"

"Minos? Well, he used to be in charge of assigning all dammed souls their proper place, but now that's all done on computers, so he isn't needed in that respect. Still, he should be able to help us, so our first destination is the second circle."

"Circle?"

"Yes, Hell is divided into ten concentric circles. Well, eleven if you count the parking lot outside, but that isn't technically considered part of hell itself."

"Oh yeah, the parking lot. What's with that, anyway?"

"Well, that is where all the rejects go. People who weren't evil enough to be sent to Hell, but not good enough to be sent to heaven either. Agnostics often end up there. Basically, it is reserved for those souls who never got off the fence and picked a side. It is always noon out there, and there is no relief from the hot sun."

"That sucks"

"Oh, things get far worse down here. Wait until you get some of the lower circle where the real sinners are punished."

"The first circle is Limbo. That's where all us heathens go. You know, those of us who didn't believe in the Big Guy. Since there are so many of us, that's the biggest circle in Hell; it extends almost endlessly in all directions from the center. Actually, I am not sure if it is a circle, at that; no one has ever explored it fully. But I digress. The next four circles are for sins of incontinence."

"Oh, okay."

"Do you know what incontinence means?"

"Uh, no," Ralph said, embarrassed.

"It didn't look like you knew. Incontinence means lack of restraint, and inability to curb one's natural urges."

"Like sex?"

"Yes, that is one. That is the one we're going to, in fact — the region of carnal sinners. There are others, though — one for gluttony, one for greed, and one for those who can't control their temper. Any of those sound like you?

"Just about all of em, actually. But what's gluttony mean?"

"Overeating."

"Oh, not that one then, I guess. But I could see myself in any of the other three."

"Mmm-hm. Well, the next one is for heretics — not too many of those come through any more, though. People don't care about religion enough to spread heresy these days. Most of the souls in there are from several centuries ago. The seventh circle is for violent sins. Most of the real sickos end up there. I have often found it ironic that those guilty of sins from this circle are made examples of in our society, while the ones from deeper circles are often rewarded with wealth and prosperity. The next two circles are for the malicious. Those who commit acts of calculated, deliberate evil. These circles are closest to Hell's heart; the most horrible punishments are delivered here. The tenth, and final, circle is where Lucifer himself resides. That's where the main office is, too.

They keep master copies of everything there. Every sin you've ever committed, every evil thought you've ever had, is on file there."

"That's scary. They know everything?"

"Certainly, but don't worry yourself over it. They have so many different souls to look after that anything they may have on you is buried so deep that no one ever looks at it unless there is reason."

"Does Minos have a file on me, too?"

"Yes, but not as extensive. Minos has access to data on just about anyone from his own computer, although he rarely uses it for that purpose. Usually he just sits and plays Doom or something on it, while his plaintiff attempts to make a case. You see, now that Minos doesn't have to assign people their place, he has set up a courthouse for souls who wish to make appeals."

"Appeals? You mean you can appeal in Hell?"

"Of course not, but some people are too stupid to understand that. Minos started it mainly as a way of amusing himself. He listens to their cries for mercy, then sends them right back without a second thought. He enjoys humiliating them.'

"Oh. How do we get there?"

"Why, public transportation , of course. All souls in Limbo get free rides. If you are ready, we may take the train to Minos right now."

Camus pointed to a staircase across from Ralph's bench. Someone had scratched "Stairway to Hell" next to it, apparently as a joke.

"Up those stairs, " Camus told him, "is an elevated train that will take us anywhere in Hell or Purgatory that we want to go. The 'El to Hell', as it has come to be known. It does not go all the way to heaven, of course, because damned souls are never allowed to see it. But it will serve more than well enough to get us around down here. Shall we go?"

Ralph shrugged his shoulders. "Now's as good a time as any, I guess. Let's roll."

With a smile and a gracious nod, Camus led Ralph up the stairs and into the next leg of their journey.

An excerpt from

The Creature

by James Freeman Hargis

The sleek black car pulled into the driveway of a large office building. Bob opened the door and dragged the two prisoners from the car. Mallion and David were still in handcuffs. Bob led them to the office building. It loomed over them. Windows lit against the pitch black sky. Somewhere a helicopter blade whirred and slapped at the air. David had never seen a building like this, but he knew what it was. It was the Megacorp command center.

The three of them walked towards the building. There were two guards at the door. The guards wore similar clothes as Bob, all black. One of the guards stopped them.

"S A Bob reporting in with prisoners," he said.

"Affirmative, proceed," said the other, stepping out of the way and opening the door.

SA Bob and his two prisoners walked down a long hall. It was brightly lit and clean. It smelled of strong potpourri and pine disinfectant, even though pines had been extinct for a long time. Doors lined the wall; there was one every ten feet or so. They came to an elevator that opened as if it were expecting them.

The three got on the elevator. There were no buttons on the walls, but the elevator moved on its own. The elevator descended, and even after they passed the sub-basement it continued to go down.

Finally, the elevator stopped and the doors opened. A short red haired girl took a step to get on the elevator, but stopped when she saw the three passengers. Her hair was long, down to a little above her knees. She was in her teens.

"Oh, excuse me," she said, startled.

"Rebecca, please step clear of the elevator," said Bob, "these two are potentially dangerous."

Rebecca stepped back from the elevator and began to look at the passengers. She did not recognize either of them, although one looked vaguely familiar. David's eyes caught Rebecca's, and he stared into her blue eyes for a moment. Bob shoved David forward. Rebecca was curious about the young man. She had never felt this way before, she had never been in love.

Bob opened a cell and forced the two prisoners into it. He slammed the barred door. He turned to Rebecca and suggested that she not converse with the two prisoners. Rebecca nodded. She got on the elevator and went up.

Bob left the two prisoners and walked into a nearby door marked "**Command Center**." The room was full of rows and rows of computers. The far wall was a monitor that had a large map of the entire Megacity. Simon McGlaughin stood at a computer console.

He was a tall, thin man. His long black hair half concealed his gaunt face and dark sinister eyes. Bob approached him.

"Sir, I have brought Mallion. I put him in a cell."

"Good, bring him to the interrogation room. I'll meet you there."

Bob returned to the cell block and opened the door to Mallion's cell. Mallion was still in handcuffs. He led Mallion into a small, hot room, and strapped him to a chair.

"Mallion," Simon began, "so nice to have you back. We were planning to erase your brain and re-program you, but first we have a problem to take care of. Tell me, how did you create the creature? More importantly, how do I stop it?"

"Creature?"

"Don't play dumb, Mallion. I know you did it."

"I don't know what you're talking about."

"Show him the tape."

A soldier at one of the many computer consoles began to push buttons. The large map of the city faded out and a video camera view of a city street appeared.

"Play," ordered Simon.

Mallion watched the screen. An SA on patrol was walking down the street. A shadow appeared behind him and slowly began to take shape. The creature came fully into view of the camera. It towered over the S A. Two huge mantis-like claws raised high above its head, below those, two muscled arms at its side. Although there was no sound coming from the video, Mallion could tell it moved silently. The slightest noise would have alerted the SA.

The creature lunged at the S A. It wrapped its four arms around the cyborg. Its muscles tightened and the SA fell into several pieces. The creature had to be very strong to shred an S A with so little effort. The creature spread two wings, which had been concealed by its massive shoulders, and flew away.

The tape ended and static snow appeared on the screen. The map then folded back into view.

"Well Mallion, I think you did it. I think you're the only one of my enemies that could have that biological knowledge. Good job. It is the perfect biological weapon, the perfect predator. Silent, strong, deadly, the perfect combination. The perfect assassin. You created it to kill me, didn't you?"

"Simon, I didn't make that thing. If I knew who did I'd tell you, but I wouldn't build that thing to kill you. I reserve that privilege for myself."

"Mallion, I think you did make it. If I were dealing with any other punk I would use torture, but I made you immune to pain, so that won't get us anywhere. You think about it. You can help me stop it, and I'll do something for you." Simon turned to one of the S A's, "Get him out of here."

"Simon, I will kill you."

They reached Mallion's cell. Mallion was still screaming at Simon, who was far out of earshot. The rusty door of the cell squeaked when it opened. Mallion was forced in, and the door was slammed shut. Mallion and David sat in silence for over an hour. Finally, David shattered the silence.

"So, what's your story?"

"I'm Mallion O'Shea, or at least I used to be. I was born in the seventh year of the forty-second century. I was an only child. I went to Sterling High School, in Sterling, Massachusetts. I graduated with honors. I left my home, which still existed in the twenty-fifth year of the forty-second century, and joined the army. I received weapons training, explosives training, martial arts, and special forces training. I flew through the ranks faster than anyone in the history of the military. By my third year I was colonel. I was assigned to assault Megacity 137. It had started a corporate uprising against the world government. Our assault failed. I was in command of thirty five elite troops. I alone survived."

An excerpt from

Beat the Storm

by Sarah Kozlowski

"We just have to beat it," I heard her whisper. "We just have to endure the storm."

Lightning tore through the rain, hitting the desert sand. Ebony and Gavin ran indoors, but I stayed outside, calling Rose. Thunder rattled windows, yet the young vampire was plastered to the ground. I finally gave up and went inside, slamming the door against the wind.

"Where's Rose?" cried Gavin, pressing against the window. "You can't leave her out there!"

Rain scratched against the windows, and the house lit up with a lighting bolt. Rose was still rooted to the ground, string into the clouds. The wind whistled through the desert, shaking the little house. Thunder crashed, and Gavin ran outside.

"Gavin, no!" I yelled, following hm. He ran to Rose, who stood surrounded by the drumming rain. A fork of lighting lashed down, slicing through the young vampire. Gavin screamed, and Rose toppled over. He knelt beside her, and I stood over them.

Rose was dead, the lighting bolt having hit her directly in the heart. Gavin screamed at the black sky, throwing insults and curses at the wind and rain. I tried to tug him inside, but he refused to leave. I ran indoors as thunder boomed ferociously.

Ebony and I solemnly watched the grief-stricken Gavin screech at the storm. The wind buffeted him, and the rain soaked him entirely. A jagged streak of white lightning brought Gavin to his knees, and another killed him. Ebony turned away from the window. I sighed sorrowfully.

"Just endure it," Ebony murmured sarcastically. "It's that simple."

Because of our raging hunger, Ebony and I fed off the blood of our dead companions. We could only drink so much before the blood turned bad, and then we were hungry once again. Ebony had grown feverish and had hallucinations, and was often muttering quietly to herself. My insanity was more subdued, and I spent all of my time staring out at the rain.

Every time the storm stopped, the Storm arrived to taunt us. We had grown to dread the halt of the falling water, but knew that there was nothing we could do. The invisible electricity around ten houses was impenetrable, and the clouds blocked the sky.

One dismal night the rain ceased almost immediately. Ebony

moaned, and I sighed softly. But instead of hearing the laughter of Norton, we first heard a very familiar voice.

"William! Where are you?"

"Oh no," I gasped, bolting out of the house, "it's Eliopulos."

Ebony and I found the mayor outside our little house, completely unharmed. He grinned when he saw us, but his smile faded as we raced towards him. The black cloud remained dry, and I knew that the Storm would be there any second.

"How did you get through the electricity?", Ebony asked, tugging Mayor Nick towards our house.

"What electricity?", he replied as we pulled him to the house.

"Just get inside, Nick?" I cried, pushing him through the door. "We can't let them find you here!"

I slammed the door as we stumbled into the house. The mortal glanced around, studied our desperate faces. "Where are Rose and Gavin? And why are you so frantic? I'm here to help!"

"They're dead," I answered, staring out the window. "And the Storm's going to show up any second. If they find you here, you're dead."

"Why didn't the electricity fry you?", Ebony demanded.

"What electricity? What are you talking about?"

Ebony turned towards me, her eyes twinkling. "Did you hear that, William? No electricity! We can run now before they put it back up!"

"No," I said, shaking my head. "It must still be up. He's mortal. Maybe it doesn't effect him like it does us."

But Ebony, for the first time in her life, wasn't listening to me. She was muttering softly to herself, a foolish grin on her face. Eliopulos was burrowing into a far corner, well away from the window. Soft laughter rang through the air, and Ebony's head jerked up.

"We must run now," she declared. "But first, I'm going to kill him."

She burst outside, giggling hysterically. Mayor Nick swore, and I went after Ebony.

"Ebony, come back!" I called. She was ignoring me, chasing after the laughter in the air. Brian Norton and the Storm were nowhere in sight, only the snickers showing their presence.

"Face me, Norton!" Ebony shrieked, darting after the traveling cackle. "I'm not afraid anymore!"

I caught up to her at last, pulling at her arm. The clouds were still dry, and I feared that the Storm could arrive at any moment. I yanked Ebony towards a house, but she threw a wild fist and knocked me to the ground. I skidded across the wet grass, my jaw throbbing. Ebony resumed her tirade at the floating laughter, edging closer to the last houses.

"I'm leaving, and you can't stop me!" she proclaimed to the sky. "Nick got through, and I will too!"

My eyes widened. I streaked towards Ebony as she floundered away from the houses. But the electricity caught her first. She shook violently, purple sparks rocketing through her. She crumpled to the cold ground, convulsing viciously.

I was still running towards Ebony when the rain began. As the first drops hit me, I knew something was different. Only when I began to burn did I realize that it was raining holy water.

I hissed, tearing at my inflamed face. I lurched away from the holy water, smashing into a door of a house and collapsing on the floor. I kicked the door closed and lay there gasping, rapidly healing.

I could hear Ebony's screams through the pounding shower of holy water. I buried my head in my hands, blocking out her anguished shrieks. They slowly died away, the sound of the rain filling the house. I hoisted myself to the window and looked out.

Ebony was gone, a few curls of black smoke her only remains. The holy water abruptly stopped falling, replaced by Brian Norton's mocking laughter.

I let out a grievous sob while falling onto the floor. Lighting flashed across the sky, and the rain began, thunder accompanying the roar of the water. Eliopulos emerged from his hiding place, cautiously moving towards me.

"William...?"

"She's dead!" I moaned. "She's dead, and there was nothing I could do!" The pouring rain muffled my sobs as it swept the last of Ebony away.

The witches had left Zane, Mayor Nick told me. They had hung around for a while, but were gone now. So the Mayor had come to find me, to tell me that I was safe. But really, the danger had never been greater.

Three great vampires were dead. Nick was helping me live, allowing me to feed from him, and I knew this put him in great jeopardy. I wouldn't let him leave the little place, lest the Storm discovered that he had aided me. If the Storm killed Nick Eliopulos, I would never forgive myself for letting him die.

The Storm no longer visited the little place, although they were still out there. They made their presence known by the constant downpour, and by Norton's occasional disembodied taunting. My insanity grew with each passing night, the tiny cage no bigger, even though I had the Mayor's company. But I was resilient, and I hung on. I refused to die.

One night, as Mayor Nick was preparing his dinner from food that we had found in the houses, the angry torrent of water stopped. The mortal looked up from his frying pan, his eyes fearful.

"I'll just crawl into a dark hole and hide," he whispered, gazing out into the silent night. I nodded, and he scamped away. First making sure Eliopulos was hidden, I strode outside.

Brian Norton stood in the center of the two streets, his black clothing blending him into the night. He wore a black fedora tipped over his face, his sunglasses gone. He smiled at me, his cold eyes glistening.

"Brayker! Good to see you're still alive," he greeted, his voice dripping with sarcasm. "I'm surprised, actually. I thought I knew your type to quit fast."

Rage boiled within me. "You don't know many things."

"Oh, really?" He chuckled, stepping closer to me. "I know more about you and your kind than you ever will. I've been watching vampires for years and years. I know your strengths, and I know your weaknesses." Norton stared me in the eye. " I know that you are going to die tonight."

I glared into Norton's eyes, for the first time seeing into his twisted soul. I knew no fear, only hate. "How old are you?" I asked, looking deep into his eyes.

His grin grew broader. "I am older than you will ever be. I am three hundred and fifty years old."

Laughter erupted from me, and Norton was taken by surprise. "Three hundred fifty?" I cried. "Rose was three hundred and fifty years old!" My laugh died away. "I am nine hundred years old. I have been through more battles and seen more blood than you could ever imagine. So do not tell me that you know when I will die. You don't know anything at all."

We were silent, Norton watching me with astonished eyes, the black clouds above us remaining dry. Finally, the witch bowed his head, his voice soft and menacing.

"I know about death, old man. I know something that you think I don't." He raised his head, his eyes boring into me. "I believe Ebony said it, before the water washed her away. Nick got through? Now that shouldn't be."

Terror struck me, and my mouth dropped. "No," I whispered.

"Yes." Norton gazed up and down the two small streets. "Now where could our friend the Mayor be?"

The witch chuckled, and I shot back into the house.

"Nick!" I yelled. "Run! Get out of here! Run before Norton—"

But I and my words skidded to a halt. Laying at my feet was

Eliopulos, a great, bleeding hole gaping from his chest. He drew short, ragged breaths, and I could hear his mutilated heart stuttering. He lifted a shaking hand towards me, and I knelt beside him.

"Oh Nick, I'm sorry—"

"William," he rasped, his voice thick with blood. "There was nothing you could have done." He gasped, his dying eyes flickering. "Beat them, William. Beat them."

His eyes drooped closed, and his worn breathing slowed. I sat there, helpless, as Nick Eliopulos sunk into death. He took his final breath, and then he was gone.

An excerpt from

Child Magic
by Hana Field

He noticed that the lighting kept casting upon the same area. "Just another thunder-storm," he thought, and continued back toward land. He didn't sail very far before he turned around and went back. Except for the full moon behind him, the sky was completely black. Something drew him to that spot; it wasn't gravitational. With the winds blowing so hard, he felt as though there was no gravity at all, and that any moment he might be thrown into the sea. But his boat kept moving closer to where the light was blinking.

There was a girl fighting for her life and she bobbed up and down the waves, as though she were part of them. She held up her hands and tried to hold up her head. But the waves were omnipotent and not nice to little girls who didn't know how to swim.

Elexander quickly tied a rope from his boat to his arm, and then dove into sea. Even under the cold water, he could still hear the pounding of the rain. It was the kind of rain that makes you wonder if it will ever stop. It was the kind everyone will soon be talking about in town, because their dogs were barking and their children couldn't sleep. The crops were ruined, and the houses flooded, trees fell, and animals were afraid to come out.

But he swam until he was able to hold her safely above water. As he held her, the lightning ceased, and he could almost see a wall of diamonds around them. He knew they were safe now, nothing could harm them, nothing could even scratch them.

That didn't mean, however, that he still didn't hear his heartbeat, or that his legs weren't numb from treading water. He was still overwhelmed by the rescue, and needed to use every muscle to make his way back to the boat. His breathing could be heard over the winds and he shivered. He still hadn't had a chance to see the magic in the girl.

The boat ride home was long, and the child had completely passed out. The only way Elexander was able to stay awake was by studying her. He saw he she was wearing the prettiest lace dress, white with all the ruffles and layers a dress could ever have. It was ruined by the water and seaweed. Elexander was oblivious.

Her face was beautiful also, even though there was a cut on one side and her hair was tangled. She was a shining star in his boat. There was a glow around her, as though she was incandescent. The glow helped Elexander find his way home safely in the dark. This was only the beginning of how she helped Elexander.

When they finally reached land, Elexander was so weak that he wanted to fall asleep right there on the beach. He could feel his knees giving in and his weight falling closer to the ground. He had to rest; he knew he had to rest. He looked up the many stairs to his door and told himself he couldn't do it. Elexander groaned and sighed and almost let the girl fall out of his arms. Her arms dangled, and a small cry was let out as her head fell back.

Another second didn't pass before Elexander quickly raced up the stairs. He figured it was like pulling off a band-aid; it hurts less if you go really fast. It was not only less hurtful on Elexander, but he knew the girl needed to indulge in warmth before she caught pneumonia. He held her tightly, as though she were gold.

At the top of the stairs, Elexander was completely drained of energy. He was beginning to feel the pain in his thighs, and his lungs felt they might burst from running, just like a soap bubble. It was still raining, and though it was less than before, he still could only see through the rain droplets. It was a struggle to open the door, and the only thing that kept him going was knowing that peace was just beyond the door.

It was peace he found in his dreams as he collapsed onto the maroon carpet.

The morning brought aches and pains to Elexander's body, and his arms were practically immobile. He could feel the throbbing veins that created his massive headache. It beat louder and faster than his heart did, digging each time with its claws deep into his head. He looked around, and the emptiness revealed why his headache was so fierce.

He first checked the bedrooms and saw no sign of anyone there. He checked the kitchen and the den, the library and dining room, and then checked the front hall. His headache didn't go away until he saw a figure pulling weeds from the garden. He walked closer and felt the familiar glow.

His thighs no longer hurt and he was able to keep his eyes wide open. For a moment, he wasn't able to move, not because of pain, but because of astonishment. The girl had managed to create an entirely new garden. It looked as beautiful as the day all the flowers started growing. There was a rainbow of flowers that grew around the large perimeter, and a fountain in the middle. Until now, everything had been dying; the flowers wept from a lack of water and began to lean over; the fountain was rusted and the drain was clogged with leaves from the peach tree. The cement was covered in dry petals and mud, the pathways were hidden by overgrown plants, and weeds were ubiquitous. It looked absolutely beautiful. It was so full of life, or maybe that was because the girl was there.

"Magic," Elexander said when she was close enough to hear.

"Hello, sir."

"Who are you?" he was completely astounded. Not all the motivation in the world could ever have embellished the garden. And here it was, so beautiful, he wished he had done it earlier.

"Who are you?" she asked.

"Elexander. How did you manage to do this?"

"It's half past noon." she answered, "I awoke and saw the garden needing some cheering up."

"We thank you. You have done a wonderful job."

"Would you mind telling me where I am?"

"Albany. Do you remember what happened last night?"

"Only a little. Will you please tell me? I'm not even sure if what I remember were dreams or not."

Elexander closed his eyes and returned to last night. He told the story as best he could, trying not to scare her. He didn't want to give her nightmares. He wanted her to find peace in Albany.

"You are welcome to stay with me," Elexander concluded. He knew if she stayed she would be nothing like the children he never wanted. She was, perhaps, more sophisticated than he was, though there must have been a few decades of age between them. He didn't think she could cause any trouble, only happiness. In fact, the more he looked at her, the more she looked like an angel rather than a little girl.

"Mind I ask where you are from?", Elexander questioned.

"Is Albany close to Dansing?" she asked.

"Yes. Dansing is very close. The town is great, but I always wonder when the war there is going to end."

"It's been going on for quite a long time, hasn't it?"

"Yes. Against Carolina."

"Oh."

The birds then flocked away and the wind stopped blowing. A silence spread over the vicinity as the drops of water were no longer heard in the fountain and the waves from the sea died out; the sun hid behind the clouds and the bees behind the flowers.

Elexander found this all to be part of the new-found magic, while the girl pretended not to notice a change.

"Well, if you're not going to tell me where you are from, would you mind sharing how it was you ended up in the wild waters?" Elexander questioned curiously. It's not that it mattered so much, that he cared, but rather he was fascinated. He wanted to know everything about her.

He wanted, in some way, to be able to show how much he was delighted by her, and he wanted her to see how much she meant to him, even though all she had been doing is smiling. But she could already see that he liked having her there, by the way his mouth turned upwards and a flame was starting to be seen in his eyes. His shoulders began to relax. The wrinkles on his forehead disappeared. He stopped clenching his teeth.

They went inside as they realized how hungry they were. The girl excitedly ran to the kitchen and offered to make the meal. After all, she was just as grateful for him as he was for her. She had never volunteered to make a meal with such excitement, or clean the garden with such delight. But she wanted to, for him. There was a force that overcame her body when she was drowning in the sea. She's not the scared little girl she used to be. Instead, she was poised and confident. She no longer needed to worry over how she should be. She just had to be.

Exhibitionism

by Ronnie Sansing

"Son of a gun," said Emeril. "That crazy intern must have left it behind." He fingered the smooth white bottle in his hands for a while and with nothing else to do, read the label. A cheesy picture of a red ant stood over the statement that read:

Caution: Hazardous to humans and pets. If swallowed, do not induce vomiting. Do not drink water or milk. Contact a physician or Poison Control Center as soon possible.

It went on to say avoid contact with skin and eyes. Emeril really saw no need for such information to be printed on the bottle. It was obvious that it was poison, so why would anyone want to ingest or touch it? It never dawned on him that someone might come across these maladies by accident. He poured some of the white powder on a small magazine table that was next to him and added a drop of coffee. As a child, he had a junior chemist set and loved to experiment with chemicals. The powder began to bubble up. As he watched the bubbles die down he looked around the room to see if there was anything else he could mix with the powder. He then eyed the bottle of flat spritzer on the table across from him.

He walked over to a table and sat down next to the bottle. The shiny cobalt wrapper was slightly torn at one of the corners, disfiguring a picture of two cheerful looking raspberries lying side by side. With the boric acid in hand, he commenced to pour the powder into the flat soda. The petal pink liquid began to come to life with bubbles and fizz. Emeril watched in awe as the drink quickly regained its effervescence. A white cap of foam began to pile up on top. The foam began to die down after a while and his concoction began to look as though it had never been flat. "Instant carbonation," he thought. Just then, he heard the intercom click on with Anna's voice.

"Emeril Clayton, please go to loading area number five. The statues have arrived." The sound of her voice ruined his karma and he made a futile attempt to rinse her words from his ears. He then got up from his merry little games and dumped the powder in the garbage.

Within a few minutes he was at the loading area. Several beefy men were pushing two large wooden crates that read "FRAGILE" and "THIS SIDE UP."

"Where is Anna?" Emeril thought as he watched the third crate being carried in. It was much smaller than the other two. A few minutes later, Anna rushed in. She seemed to be out of breath.

"Where were you?" he asked impatiently.

Anna, in an accusing manner, retorted, "Where were you? You took so long to get here I went down to the staff lounge to get you, but you weren't there. Then I went back to the office to see if you'd stop by there..."

"I was on my way up here. You could have waited. I swear, you're so impatient sometimes. What's up with you today, anyway? You're more pissed off than usual."

"Pissed off? Pissed off? I'll tell you why I'm pissed off. Number one: you changed my plans without permission and therefore the statues got here late. Number two: I have to work overtime with you. Number three..."

"And number three," interjected one of the moving men, "we only have time to move one of these statues tonight, so stop your whining and let's get a move on. We'll be back early in the morning to finish the rest." Emeril held back the need to applaud this brave man.

Flabbergasted, Anna quickly shut up and supervised as the men set one of the statues into place over in the exhibit hall. It was one of the larger statues. It was a sinewy horse made of bits of wood and foam peanuts. Emeril thought it was one of the ugliest things he had ever seen. He appreciated art, but there was no way he could appreciate this. After the movers had left, Anna and Emeril headed back to the office. Emeril noticed that Anna was looking a bit peevish. Her eyebrows were strenuously furrowed together and her eyes a bit watery. Every five seconds or so, she'd stifle down a painful belch.

"What's wrong with you?" he inquired. "You're not looking so hot."

She stifled down another wave of gas and managed to say, "Nothing. Just a little indigestion, I think."

Emeril was still a bit concerned. She really looked sick. Could he be feeling sorry for the little vixen? "Well, go home and take a bicarb. I'll be around the office later. Gotta go get my food out of the lounge. I left it there, so hopefully the ants didn't get to it yet." He parted from Anna and watched her get into the elevator. He had a slight fear of the contraption and took the back steps to the third floor.

On his way down, he passed a melange of the construction workers' mess. An open sack half full with quick drying cement mix, a couple of dirty tools, and a wheelbarrow holding cement that was just starting to dry. He made a mental note to talk to the workers about their messy ways. When he got to the lounge, he went to the magazine, picked up the last Ho-Ho and threw away the now tepid coffee. He looked around the lounge at the cleared tables and the slightly out of place plastic red chairs. He turned off the lights and closed the door.

The muffled pat of Italian leather slippers on cold, hard concrete filled the back stairwell as Emeril trudged back to his office. The soft tread on the lavender Berber carpet greeted his feet as he entered the hallway. When he finally reached his office, a jarring jolt of static nipped his fingertips, making his slightly graying hair stand on end as he touched the metal frame of the doorway. Slightly shaken, he walked in and viewed Anna face down on her desk, like a kid who'd fallen asleep during math class. A mass of curly red hair blanketed her head like an angora rug. Cat nap? It couldn't hurt to wake her up. He took his slightly buzzed hand and placed it on her left shoulder padded clavicle. Even through all that material, she felt as small and frail as a sick child. He then gave her a hearty shake.

"C'mon, Anna. Wake up. I gotta head outta here." No reply. He shook her once more and watched the tangled curls jostle around with the sway of her body. She felt quite limp. "Anna? Are you feeling okay? Maybe I should drive you home or some..." His sentence was caught short by a rose colored twinkle in his right visual field. It was a bottle of raspberry spritzer with a quarter of an inch of beverage left inside. The blue wrapper was torn at the corner, just like the one in the lounge. Exactly like the one in the lounge. Emeril felt a wave of cold sweat flush over him as reality smacked him in the face like an abusive lover. It was the same bottle. The one with the boric acid. Anna must have left it there and picked it up when she was looking for him. No wonder she was feeling so sick.

"Aw, Anna. Tell me you didn't drink the stuff. Tell me you didn't." He took her by the shoulder and leaned her face up in the chair. Her skin had gone dove white and foam trickled from her tiny ruby lips. Emeril had never seen a dead person, but in his book, she was as good as gone. She wasn't breathing and he had no idea how to take a pulse. A strange feeling went through him. It was that if-only-I-hadn't feeling. A time you should have looked, but didn't. "Anna, didn't you even taste something funny?!" he yelled. "What in the world am I doing?" he thought. "I'm talking to a corpse. What's next?" Instinct told him to call security and 911. Common sense told him to dump the body. Who'd ever believe that he had poisoned her by accident. He then heard a little voice in his head tell him something that his mother always told him: If you have common sense, then you have all the sense in the world. Emeril would have to get rid of the body.

A Small Town Called Pasad

by Pete Steadman

James decided to be sure that he read that paper right, and stopped a man who was taking a morning stroll with his wife.

"Hey, do you know the date today?", James asked.

"Tuesday, May 1..." The rather overweight man cheerfully replied.

"No, no. I mean the year." James quickly added.

The man now gave James a peculiar look. "1972...Say, are you that guy who was at Davey's Bar last night?", the man asked.

"Uhhh...Yeah, I was there last night."

"Wait here for a second, please. Somebody wants...to talk to you..." the man said.

The pudgy man hurried off with his wife, and minutes later returned with a neatly dressed man in a suit and a balding head. This guy was short and frail, using a cane to walk. The guy in the suit thanked the pudgy guy and his wife, and instructed them to leave. They did.

"Let's go for walk...James, is it?" the man motioned James to follow.

"How do you know my name?", James asked.

"Just listen. First of all, I don't talk to just anybody in this town. I am the mayor, you know, and I feel compelled only to talk to outsiders. Now, I'm sure you think this town is a pretty weird place, but I'll explain, and hopefully you'll understand. Now, the leaders of this town, myself included, came here twenty years ago, and were just as confused as you probably are now. Everything seems old, and confusing, and believe me, I know." James nodded. "For some reason, time moves slower here. You've been here for one night, and that one night is equal to maybe one week outside of this town."

"Anyway, me and my colleagues saw this as great opportunity to live...longer. After a week or so in this town, we realized how great it would be to keep this town the way it is. We could live longer, and live easier. There aren't as many taxes to pay here, as compared to out there, for instance. So, over the twenty years we've been here, we managed to gain complete control over this place. I am now mayor, and am the one who is forced to give the order to kill those who don't cooperate. We keep it the way it is. All outsiders who stumble in are watched constantly, and if they try to tell people on the outside, they are, to put it bluntly, killed. Most people aren't allowed back outside, but some exceptions are made on that. Basically, what I'm trying to ask you, is will you cooperate?" He looked to James for an answer.

"Sir-"

"John…" the man interrupted.

"John, I feel that the people here should have the freedom to explore other options. It's just not right to keep people here, or kill innocent people for trying to tell people the truth," James said. John hesitated and then smiled.

"You're absolutely right, James. We'll tell the people tomorrow."

John then offered a handshake, which James reluctantly accepted, and then the two parted ways. James wondered how that could have been so easy, and decided that the whole encounter was…creepy. He decided he would leave early the next day.

The rest of James' day was spent in his motel room, lazily watching TV. He went to bed early, and had a hard time falling asleep.

Almost three hours after he turned his lights off, he heard his door quietly creak open. Two people whispered in brief conversation, not at all audible to James, who stayed still, pretending to be asleep.

Seconds later, he felt cold, sharp steel touch his throat. James quickly rolled over and punched the man nearest to him between the eyes and slammed the man's hand against his knee, forcing the obviously muscular, black ski-mask wearing man to drop his knife. James plowed over the other, skinnier man, and bolted out the door into the street.

James was running for all he was worth, but the two men were still gaining on him. "Dammit!" he thought. "I should've kept my mouth shut in front of that Mayor!" James was angry at himself for not figuring out that it was probably the mayor who had his room searched, and that the Mayor ordered these two guys to kill him.

James wheezed as he felt his heart beating faster than a cheetah on speed. He mumbled a curse for smoking since the age of twelve. He could see that he had to get off the straight road he was on, because the mayor's henchmen were obviously better sprinters. He tried to avoid thinking about what kind of pain they would inflict upon him before they actually killed him.

Suddenly, out of the corner of his eye, James saw a chance. About 40 yards west of the grassy prairie surrounding the road was forest. The heavy thicket of trees combined with the darkness of night would make for easy hiding and hard hunting. James mustered all of his remaining energy for the final sprint to the woods.

James' fatigue had forbade him to notice how close the henchmen really were to him and, just as he began his final sprint, a heavy, calloused hand crashed down on his shoulder.

The energy mustered for the run to the woods was now overpowered by a furious instinct to stay alive. James frantically shouted, pushed, pulled, spat, bit, and punched until he broke free from the grip of the much stronger henchmen.

James somehow managed to reach the forest, and the henchmen gave up pursuit, realizing it would be impossible to find anybody in the cover of the pitch black woods during the night. James felt safe for the time being as he pressed further into the woods and sat on a rock, letting his heart return to its normal pace. A fire burning in him told him to go confront the mayor, turn his people against him. Tell them the truth. His instinct told him to hike to the next town over, and forget the whole incident. As he closed his eyes, he decided he was going to that town, and get revenge on the mayor. He smiled as his thoughts drifted to dreams.

Untitled

by Victoria Maldonado

Patient Journal
Julian Green

Comments:
Journal was unsolicited and discreetly monitored. Patient gave far
greater insight to his condition through the written format, especially
when allowed to type, than in human contact sessions. However, further computer dependence was deemed unhealthy and keyboard contact was terminated.

August 12, 1996

*They have not let me near anything "dangerous" in a long time. I have to
take all of the letters and move them to a different hiding place or they will find
them. I will hide too, where they won't find me. Hide. Now. Here are the
letters. I hope they don't fall out where I hide this. Here they are:*

Marley-

*My lizard's name is Glenda. Glenda the Gecko. She's my personal
muse. I got her one day a year ago from a pet shop about to get busted for ille-
gal animals, because I couldn't afford the cheetah. She turned out to have been
bred in captivity for several generations, so I couldn't really return her to the
wild. Plus, I didn't know where she came from originally. I got her the same
day my MIT application was accepted and I met one of my best friends, so she's
officially Glenda the Good Witch of the North.*

*You never said what you thought about hacking and you didn't answer how
you got into my room. How do you know me if you're not online?*

*I guess I'll just leave that alone for now. What books have you read? Why
do you like them? I loved marine biology, mostly deep-sea life. Maybe physics
is a more noble and abstract art to you. Well, the phone's ringing so I'll go.*

Julian

Julian–

I think "hacking" is a pointless occupation for you to have, Julian,
and I'm upset that you make your so-called career out of it. Now
physics, physics is beautiful. I don't believe in God, but I believe that
the laws of physics operate on the same level, that they were not created by a divine being, but actually are one, as far as the term "being" can

have meaning in that context. What I think of marine biology is rather neutral. I don't have anything in particular against it for others, but I don't like it myself. It describes; it is introspection on the part of the people who practice it. It doesn't tell us anything we didn't already know. It doesn't create anything, any new concepts. It simply accumulates facts. It is a totally inexact science, like biology in general. Your mind is capable of much more than that. The intuitive mathematical abilities you were blessed with are totally applicable to physics, but you choose not to apply them there. It's disheartening.

Marley

But Marley, isn't the science of chaos applicable to biology? Can't it be used to further chaos studies, which can help us understand physics better? Don't you believe that the larger picture, when examined in detail, must contain the smaller?

Julian, you dolt, that's obvious. Physical laws govern all interaction, and yield all answers. Once the physical laws are determined and unified, they will explain "chaos," not the other way around. Physics describes the fish in their motions and structures, as well as the planets and stars.

Marley -- you believe that there is no random action, no free will? The mind is in no way divorced from the body and the brain? How can you survive like that? How can you exist thinking that nothing you think is really your own?

All thought arises from a certain randomness of electron motion, the particle wave in every atom of every molecule in every cell in your conglomeration of nerves, so thoughts may be random but not your own, on purely physical terms. I exist every day with this truth, and I survive it with the knowledge that existence is unnecessary but inevitable, that it travels on into infinity until the end of all things. When all the energy is expended and all the particles are evenly distributed and the universe is a blank mass of deadness. Whether or not I can think is an absolutely moot point.

Jesus, Marley! Jesus Christ! God! I mean, God...What kind of world do you live in? How does your head work to sustain that? How in hell do you manage to survive thinking you are nothing? I mean, nothing?

Poor Julian. Even the atheist, the agnostic, and you will run to God when faced with something larger than yourself. It is only a belief I hold, an idea that is my rock solid conviction, but you have to turn to beings nonexistent and higher than you to cope. It's a matter of ego. It's pure ego, your sense of self obscuring the knowledge. And you know what? God doesn't matter either.

Marley

Humankind is scum. I got you, Marley. Fine. I guess you can think whatever you want. But how do you integrate your total lack of caring with Sally Struthers and the starving children? Do you give them money because money doesn't matter anyway, or do you keep it from them because no one cares? Are you a democrat or a republican? Should we save the rainforests or burn them? Or are you just too cold to care either way?

I guess it's the latter for me, Julian my boy. Apathy is the only recourse of those who have no souls. Or righteous indignation, in your case. Attach is the last defense of the cornered mind, the weak mind, the foolish mind, just like the cornered rat. Are you a rat, Julian? Is blind refutation all you can manage?

Julian, I see you've been silent for a few days. I don't know whether you are thinking over what I've said, or are completely ignoring me from here on out. The latter, most likely, so I'll stop too. If you wish to stop behaving like the child you are, then respond whenever you wish with some intelligent piece of your own random electron waves.

Marley, isn't intelligence rather weak and arbitrary in itself? What's the point of having it if existence is so pointless? Why do you care about physics or what I do or the non-contributing spirit of biology, if all of that will lose meaning when there is nothing left?

Still dithering in an effort to compete, I see, but at least putting some effort into it. In answer, I can only say that the cards fell wrong for humans, and they still strive to know their "place in the universe," to understand everything. When a person has the capability to contribute greatly and chooses not to, like you, it strikes a human reaction in my mind. I'm upset. I want to know my fate, inside and out, before it happens to me, and I believe that I can insofar that since I am nothing, I must be everything, since everything is nothing too.

Come again, my friend? It's an interesting contrast, I suppose. But what about the creators, the artists, the writers you value so much?

You couldn't comprehend a really interesting contrast if you could identify one, my dear Julian. Don't hurt your head.

Either you are dimmer than I thought you were and are not comprehending my message regarding rats, or you have become sincere in your questions. I'll give you the benefit of the doubt.

A true creator understands what I know, that nothing matters at all. Many of them ache over this knowledge, but I do not begrudge them their ache.

When they create art, music, words, they are not trying to communicate the ache, but the concept, that the artist and the viewer and the art are nothing. The creator creates in the knowledge that he or she can do no such thing. The fact that they can comprehend and articulate this idea is what draws my respect.

Not like you, Julian. You who have only questions, no answers, no beliefs. You who understand nothing and create nothing. You earn my disgust, and that's all.

Marley, I'm sorry. I just wasn't that good at physics, okay? I started losing control of the concepts and I couldn't grasp the material anymore. Now I'm really good with computers. I can't help it. And you said you weren't that good at music or art either. It can't really matter if you're just not good at something, can it? Like, I'm not good at believing that I mean nothing to nobody.

Julian looks calm as he sits down, the lizard resting neglected in the corner of the room. He tosses his hair back over his shoulder, then tucks it behind his ears. He extends his long hands over the keyboard, and begins to write. He knows that he must keep himself safe from those who would hurt him where he's going, and he types faster, finding a rhythm somewhere in his brain as he understands what he has to do.

Somewhere in his mind, below all of the functions and cares, the knowledge of the language of human information, rests something that will not stay still for long. Stirring discontentedly, its motions disappearing into the strength of Julian's concentration. Though submerged it is there, unhappy, demanding. Julian smiles, oblivious to his own mind, and begins to find his way through the organized data left by the human race, documenting itself to the towers that glow in his head, the towers that are protected carefully and maniacally from him and others like him. They are not that hard to find, and he does not make the pretense of asking permission as he slips through the wall of the densest one, through tiny cracks of his own making, to this place which he has tested carefully for faults, holes, defenses. He ignores doors, windows, mortar, phasing through the bricks, keys clattering as his heart jumps into his throat and he is inside. He is disguised as nothing and as nothing he changes everything, solely because he can and because he thinks that one, one watching him will see him and come back. He creates perfect beauty in his path and the programs that represent him stand as David's, but the watcher isn't watching and doesn't understand.

A small man in a huge basement spills his coffee and nearly has a heart attack while he is cast in the same light as the boy, trying to stop what he watches from actually occurring, contacting all the help he has and still losing.

Row after row of quiet computers in a long, white building stop computing their normal tasks and begin to reconfigure themselves just as quietly.

Several confused children begin reading about an open universe and an end to all things as they search for information on their country's executive processes as controlled from its capital.

As the economy swings wildly for a half hour, stocks exhibit never-before-seen trends seemingly in fast motion, the Federal Bank of the United States suddenly has no history, no background, no records, no money, and no future as it sinks into the prediction of a heatless death and a flashing cursor.

Twenty-nine minutes and three seconds later the tsunami pulls back as quickly as it came, returning the shore to relative normality, the foundations of the civilization that makes its home there only subtly shaken. Somewhere a boy is laughing. Laughing with pure joy in a comfortable chair in a darkened room. The eerie light of his computer his only companion.

An excerpt from

Schemes

by Edward Peterson

"People are stupid," George had said. That's not necessarily the case. However, although not all people are stupid, many are ignorant. Not that ignorance is always bad, either. If you live in a society of ignorant people, as we do, it can be just fine. Provided, of course, no knowledgeable people enter the fold.

George was ignorant. He had invested so much time into our plan that he was utterly ignorant of the possibility that anything other than what he planned could happen.

The idea of betraying George and Dave occurred to me early on. About a day before the incident at George's apartment, I had just finished my initial calculations on the division of the money and I was looking at the paper where I'd scrawled it all down.

$$\$1,160,800$$
$$-\quad 30,000$$
$$\text{-----------}$$
$$\$1,130,800/2 = \$565,400$$

$565,400. That number stared back up at me.

The problem with money is that you always seem to think of it in relation to any other sums you've encountered recently. For instance, to someone who's only got $20 in their pocket, a sum of over five hundred thousand dollars would be mind blowing. But to me, someone who would soon have access to more than a million, it was shamefully low.

I looked back up at the top. $1,160,800. And then, just like that, the idea was in my head. To take it all for myself. I thought it I over for a little while. I could probably get away with it. Especially if I could arrange a head start somehow...say, by having them hide the money and not come back for it till after the weekend. Plenty of time to double back, get it, and be thousands of miles away by the time Monday rolled around. I could do it. So, I would.

Don't think of this as a horrible deed. They were criminals, you know. It wasn't as if it was their money I was stealing. They wouldn't lose anything of their own except the few weeks of wasted effort they'd put into the scheme.

No, they were criminals. Convicted felons. (Well, actually, I'm not sure if Dave was ever convicted, but he had been arrested a few times.)

I was a second class thief at best. In a pinch, I could fall back on an old code of honor, saying, for justification: "Only steal from thieves." That was what I was doing. Both in double crossing my partners and in the actual scheme itself. The money wasn't really Scheider's either. He, too, was a thief. In fact, a grand jury recently agreed, unanimously, in federal court.

Besides, being criminals, the two of them would probably pull some other job to take the place of the one they'd been cheated out of.

And even if they didn't, and then never made another ill gotten profit, what would that mean? Dave would have to leave the occupation that was driving him at 80 m.p.h. towards a nervous breakdown. And George would never open his liquor store. All the people in his neighborhood wouldn't be cheated out of their hard earned dollars by his exorbitant prices, and wouldn't have alcohol so close on hand. Maybe a few of them would even sober up.

Yeah, it was really a win–win situation. Secure in my eminent million, I kicked back and began to laugh.

Weeks later, after the final briefing at the McDonald's, I returned to work. I signed in with an elaborate and almost illegible signature and grinned all the way to my desk. Once there I abruptly stopped. *Nothing conspicuous, Nick*, I reminded myself.

I checked the wall clock. It was 2:30. That left two and a half hours till I could go home. Two and a half hours left in this career. Two and a half hours left in this *life*.

Briefly, I wondered what would happen after I left tonight. I wouldn't be noticed as missing until I failed to show up for work on Monday. Someone would call the police, no doubt, and there would be an investigation. The cops would search my house, my desk...no clues there. I'd checked.

Then they'd interview my co-workers. And they'd hear about the same, dull drone of a worker that everyone thought of Nick Keaton being by now. As long as I didn't do anything to overshadow it in the next couple of hours, that image, cultivated over the course of three years, would be the one that stuck with people.

All the cops would discover was that a dedicated bank employee who nobody knew very well had simply vanished off the face of the Earth. Nothing would link that with any robbery, because if all went well, no one would ever know anything had been stolen.

What then? I wondered. Eventually, I supposed, someone would have me declared legally dead and cash in on my minuscule life insurance policy. They'd get maybe $20,000 (I wasn't sure if I'd paid all the premiums) while I got away with over a million. Who'd do it? Maybe

George...if he could find a way to link himself to me without revealing the nature of our business partnership.' Yes, there was a certain irony in that...$20,000 to the master planner, $1,200,000 to the accountant.

$20,000...we were gonna pay the *lackey* more than that!

I felt the urge to laugh again, but suppressed it.

Anyway, I had a few more things to do here. Dull, menial jobs consistent with my drone image. Three new accounts chock full of numbers to be entered into the database. Accounts opened by people with jobs just as boring as mine, probably.

My wanderer's spirit was growing. Even as I entered the data, I questioned the nature of accounts in general. The principal of opening a bank account, as I saw it now, was giving your money to someone else. To hold for you, mind you, but giving it away nonetheless. Leaving it in their hands. In one place. For decades, maybe. That was what opening an account meant. And after three years of overseeing the process, I was now opposed to the entire thing. When I got the Scheider money, I was going to keep it with me at all times. Where I cold hold it in my hands, and be secure in my possession. Putting it in a bank went totally against that. You are putting it in someone else's hands, and it was only as secure as the bank. And I, of all people, knew how easily a bank could be robbed.

An excerpt from

Something I Lost
by Paul Giedraitis

She sat on his couch and ran her fingers through her hair. Her hair had a certain sheen to it, a glow, that made it flow red like wildfire. She pulled her lighter from her purse and lit a cigarette.

The apartment was luxurious; crystal vases, waxed floors, oak furniture, chandeliers, fireplace, the whole deal. She looked across the room at the thing she had brought for him. It was some kind of statuette; beautiful; extravagant. To her it looked like one of those ancient Greek goddesses; powerful, majestic; invincible.

Lion came from the kitchen and sat next to her. She smiled primly.

"Tangueray," he said, stopping short. She looked so sexy the way she sat, legs curled up, hair draped elegantly around her face, erotic smile, eyes that were pure, yet dangerous. She answered.

"Yes, love?"

Lion smiled. "Tangueray, I have a simply fabulous idea. Let's make some midnight margaritas."

She grinned and took a drag from her cigarette; "Sure. Lion, I--"

"What flavor, love? Strawberry is fantastic, but pineapple is equally good. Oh, drat, the blender isn't plugged in..."

Tangueray got up and walked to him. She put her hand on his neck and sighed.

"Something wrong, love?" he asked.

"Well," she said, and paused. The weight of what she was about to say loomed over her.

"What, love?" he grinned. "Come on, spit it out."

"It's... about your wife."

"Oh, her. Don't worry, Tangueray, she's gone. It's only you and I, now." He took her hands in his and kissed her on the lips. She smiled.

"But how, I mean who did you, I mean, what happened to her?"

Lions eyes became serious; "I'm going to be honest with you, love." He paused. "My wife is dead."

She was stunned.

"But how--"

"I had her killed. Icepick. That was the fellow's name, I think."

"Icepick? You mean the mob boss? He's dangerous, Lion. I don't want you associating with people like that. Did you pay him for it?

Killing her, I mean."

"That's the beauty of it," he said, smiling again, almost insane with glee. "I didn't. Well I was going to, you see, but I was thinking, if we left town, no one will be the wiser. And I'll, I mean we'll, be $50,000 richer. So do you want strawberry or pineapple?"

Tangueray stepped back. She felt distant from him now, as if Lion had suddenly become a monster.

It was because of her. His wife was dead and it was all because of her.

"This is no joke, Lion. I don't want you dead over something like this. If you don't pay Icepick, he'll mark you for death. He'll just as soon kill you as he would anyone else."

"Everything is going to be just fine, love. I can promise you that. Everything is going to be just fine."

Tangueray picked up her purse and walked to the door.

"Take care of yourself, Lion. I'll call you tomorrow."

"You're leaving."

"I have to." She kissed him passionately on the lips.

"Bye, love."

Tangueray left the apartment and headed for the elevator. She headed into the cool night, passing a large man in a suit wearing a pair of mirrored sunglasses on her way out.

Section Five

Brown Flowers

opposite:
linoleum cut by
Megan Iwamuro, age 17

"Theatre Geek"

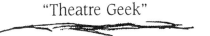

I am a theatre geek,
proud and true,
let me do my call for you.
I love Albee,
he twists my mind,
and Miller makes me understand suicide.
Willy Loman,
a dead salesman,
and that "Zoo Story,"
with Jerry,
the crazy person.

"A Crucible" with witch trials,
"A Price" with memories in an old house,
and a single feeling of cynicism behind it all.
Modern plays twist that mind,
taking me to a whole new side

But let's go back,
yes Sir and Madam,
to Shaw and Pygmalion.
Eliza Doolittle,
learning to talk,
what a preposterous thought!
Making street trash into royalty,
"My dear that sounds fine with me!"

Going back,
further now,
Shakespeare and Jonson,
rule Britain town.
They are said to be the best,
of all time,
giving us "Hamlet, "
"The Alchemist,"
and poetry of renown.
"Making Much Ado About Nothing"
in the comedy,
known as life,
and keeping the background lively,
with minstrels on fife.

Bringing spectacle to height,
motion to stage, the stage, ahh, the stage,
alive with the human history of man,
heightened realism by the devious playwright;
striking the audience as insignificant,
for the moment,
but remains,
behind the scenes,
as the true God.

Dedicated to Ewing Eugene Baldwin.

Gina M. Holechko

We acknowledge the following apprentice writers for their one-act plays which, due to space limitations, are not printed in full.

We Acknowledge:

Natasha Achanzar, for *Almost Naked*. Nina, a conflicted teenage girl who has been "good" all her life, makes a decision to act out at a party, getting drunk and removing her shirt for a boy she doesn't know. Her boyfriend learns of this and leaves her, causing Nina to have a breakdown.

G.M. Holechko, for *Best Laid Plans*. Marie, hoping to rekindle romance, plans an elaborate dinner for her old boyfriend Paul, who has gone on to college, only to find that Paul has completely changed and no longer cares for her. She is consoled by her mother and learns something about herself in the process.

Amber Wilson, for *Carmilla's Angst*. Carmilla, seemingly carefree, hangs out with her friends, wisecracking about the people around them, each episode ending with, "Is your mom dead yet?" This finally leads to Carmilla's confrontation with her emotional pain over her dying mother.

Lauren Nicole McLemore, for *Love Lasting*. Marissa, struggling to survive in a battling family, contemplates getting pregnant in order to "have someone to love". Her parents, learning of her plan, reluctantly talk with her and apologize for their detachment, vowing to love her.

Reyna Pena, for *When the Shield Breaks*. Esperanza, waiting for friends to come to a party in her home, confronts her father's racism toward blacks, only to have the conflict literally brought home: two uninvited black men come to her party, incensing her father. Father and daughter are forced to deal with one another.

Caryn Bryant, for *Rings*. Alexandria encounters Grady, an elderly street person and a former employee of her grandfather's, who was fired from his job when her father took over the business. The unlikely pair form a bond, which her father hastily and unsuccessfully attempts to break through intimidation.

Brian Boers, for *Michael*. Michael, a young boy, resists the attempts of his mother's boyfriend to make friends with him, hating the way the man strains to be friendly, even fatherly. At dinner, the mother announces she is getting married, setting off a confrontation of wills.

An excerpt from
Brown Flowers
By Yvonne B. Pitts

Brown Flowers, by Yvonne B. Pitts. Sable, a young black girl and gifted poet, struggles for recognition in a family uninterested in poetry. Her sister Sybill mocks her poetic nature, calling it her "Ms. Mysterious" persona. Sable tries to convince Sybill to lead a more meaningful life, especially to avoid Peeve, a seemingly rough street character. Sable's blunt mother, Asha, spends her days watching television and being waited on hand and foot by the sisters. Sable holds her own within the family battling. Peeve watches Sable dance through her bedroom window and becomes interested in her. Asha's common-law husband, Chuck, comes home from work and demands to be waited on, bringing the drama to a climax.

SABLE'S VOICE: Slowly, I'm falling in love with myself.

(Lights up. Stevie Wonder's song, "Love's In Need" is playing loudly in the girl's room. Sable is reciting a poem in front of the bureau mirror. Sybill is lying down on the full bed talking on the phone about something obviously funny. She's wearing black- jeaned bell bottoms with a red and white blouse. Sable is wearing faded blue Khaki shorts and a dingy Pro-Afro t-shirt. Her hair is in six cornrow braids.)

SYBILL(on the phone): Girl, I'd never put twigs in my hair...I mean it's bad enough she's black as hell, but on top of that she's got nappy hair! I mean...my hair's nappy(she feels her hair), but it's soft and soft looking.

SABLE(abruptly): You need to get your soft and curly haired butt off the phone and help clean up this room. (She picks up a broom from against the wall and begins sweeping.)

SYBILL(continuing conversation): There's no way in the world a perm could repair that forest...maybe, lye or acid would help.

SABLE: Maybe if I poured some lye or acid on you, you'd get off that damn phone!

SYBILL(frustrated): Listen, China, I have to go. You really should talk to your friend, though...about that do wop grease mop on her head! (She hangs up phone and sits up on the bed.) I'm getting sick of you interrupt hangs up phone and sits up on the bed.) I'm getting sick of you interrupting my conversations, you need to get some business.

SABLE(calmly): I've got business.(She grinds the broom into the floor)

SYBILL: Humph. I can't tell, seems like you're always in mine. I need to get out of this house.

SABLE: Get out then! I like your audacity...it's not like you do anything around here anyway.(She sweeps violently)

SYBILL: Momma never asked me to do anything.

SABLE: You never volunteer! All you do is yap on the phone!

SYBILL: That's my business! What I do is my business.

SABLE: No, it's not.(She sweeps closely to SYBILL's bed, whacking the springs) Not when you're living in a house with other people. You're supposed to help out, too.

SYBILL: Damn! Do I ever complain about your gypsy dancing or that jive you jabber? (She mimics SABLE in front of the mirror.) I want to feeel him under my skin...I want to bathe in his warmth and securiiiity...(She flings herself on the bed.)

SABLE(sarcastically): I don't feel that way about Peeve.

SYBILL(laughing to herself): Or anyone else.

SABLE: You don't know what I feel. (She begins sweeping trash into a pile.)

SYBILL: I have a good idea. Your "Ms. Mysterious" persona doesn't phase me one bit. You're no different from anyone else.

SABLE: See, that's what your problem is. You can't except the fact that I AM different from EVERYBODY else and I like it that way. (She spins around facing Sybill) So Bam!

SYBILL: Bam my butt! (She gets up and walks to mirror, proceeds to brush hair.)Maybe, if you don't act like you're so-what they call it? Uhmm- bourgeois, you could get some friends.

SABLE: I've got friends, and you know what, they're real friends... and I'm real, too. (She walks over to Sybill, facing her side) When have you ever known me to fake anything? Don't get me confused with you; we're two totally different peaches.

SYBILL: So what you trying to say? (She faces Sable)

SABLE: Don't step in the trash.

SYBILL(Smacking her lips): Sometimes, you really amuse me.

SABLE: Peeve's trash, rather.(She detaches dustpan from broomstick)

SYBILL: There you go again, meddling in my business. (She sits back down on her bed) I've got Peeve taken care of.

SABLE: Hell, no you don't. Who is he? Really, you don't even know who he is. (She sweeps trash onto dustpan.) Do you?

SYBILL: I know he's the finest guy that's ever lived, and once I get him-he's mine. (She crosses over to the window.) I don't care what I have to do.

SABLE: Why do you always go for those wanna-be cool, gangbanging, no-good, lying chaps? (She dumps trash in wastepaper basket) Not just guys around here, but those false girls you run with? (She looks defiantly at SYBILL.) You're the one who needs friends. (A loud, harsh voice calls SABLE from offstage.) Coming, mama! Damn, what does she want now?   (She stomps out the room, SYBILL slumps down by the window.)

LIGHTS DOWN

SABLE'S VOICE: A kiss, a drip, an open wine bottle (Lights up in living room. Asha is lying down on the couch smoking a cigarette. She's wearing blue baggy jeans, a large Pepsi t-shirt, and tan house shoes. A door slams. Sable comes rushing in.)

SABLE(panting): Ma'am?

ASHA(watching TV): I need you to get some stuff from the store. Ummm..some liver cheese, two packs of crackers, and orange juice, the forty cent bottle.

SABLE: But, Mama, I just went to the store.

ASHA: So, you're going again. (She taps her cigarette ashes on the floor)

SABLE: Why do you put the ashes on the floor?(gesturing towards ashtray) The ashtray's right there and nothing's in it.

ASHA(leaning over and tapping ashes into tray): Now there is. Since you have so much to say and so much to question, how about getting that dust out the window sill and emptying the garbage? Yeah, and empty the ashtray.

SABLE(mumbling to herself): I always clean the windows, always empty the ashtray, always go to the store, always doing stuff. (She picks up ashtray from table and empties it)

ASHA: I hear you jabbering, you supposed to...

SABLE(interrupting): I do everything around here! (She slams down the empty ashtray)

ASHA: No you don't. You don't run the house or pay the bills. (She takes a long drag off her cigarette)

SABLE: You don't either! Chuck does the real housekeeping and you don't even appreciate him.

ASHA(getting up from the couch):Don't you dare stick that narrow nose of yours in my business. You stay out a dat.

SABLE: OUCH! (She feigns to have burned her mouth) My lips burning!

ASHA(laying back down on the couch): You don't amuse me. (SYBILL enters)

SABLE: I need some air. (She walks over to window, pulls back curtains, and looks out.)

ASHA: Get all the air you can get, after you get my things from the store and clean that dirty window your looking out of.

(SYBILL rushes out and rushes back in with a bottle of windex and paper towels, hands items to SABLE with a smile.)

SABLE(to SYBILL): At least I can't say you've never done anything for me.

SYBILL(plopping down on the couch beside ASHA): I'll do anything for you...sister.

SABLE: Well, how about going to the store for Mama?

SYBILL: I said for you.

ASHA: But, I'm yo' Momma. You should want to do for me without question.

SYBILL(sighing): Whatever, Mama.

ASHA: Don't you agree? (She taps her cigarette ashes on the floor)

SYBILL: Yeah.

ASHA(to SABLE): Get me my change purse. (Sable hesitates, then gives ASHA small, black pouch from off the TV set.)

SABLE: Sybill should go, I always go to the store.

SYBILL(getting up and walking to mirror): Sybill can't go to the store, not today. (She removes a lip liner from her pocket and begins to draw her lips) I'm on a mission today.

SABLE: You're always on a mission...for whom is this one for?

SYBILL: That's none of your business, and the only person I'm ever on a mission for is myself.

SABLE: Yourself, and somebody else. (Phone rings loudly. Sybill rushes over to table and answers.)

SYBILL(on phone): Hello? (Obvious deflection in voice) Oh, hey Jherma...yeah...where did you see him? (She slides down the wall onto the floor.)

ASHA: Get off the wall! You know how dry white walls pick up dirt! (SYBILL crawls away from wall and sits on the floor.)

SABLE(to ASHA): Must be talking about that no-good Peeve. (She scoots back in window sill, holding windex and paper towels.)

ASHA(lighting another cigarette): How you know he's no-good?

SABLE(looking over her shoulder out the window): I can tell by the way he walks down the streets and leans to the side when he talks to people. I think he's just a phony, always talking loud and don't mean a thing he's talking about...

ASHA(interrupting): There you go, making assumptions about people...passing judgement on folks.

SABLE: I'm not passing judgement...

ASHA?(interrupting again): Don't dispute my word! That's another bad problem you have.

SABLE: How is stating my opinion a bad problem?

ASHA: Disputing my word is a problem, and your opinion is bad. So, keep your bad mouth shut and your opinions to yourself.

SABLE: I will.

ASHA:SHUT UP!(SABLE jumps, dropping windex.) Now, don't you waste that, windex cost money! (SABLE scoots out window sill bumping into brown flower vase; it falls over) Pick..pick em up...

(SYBILL's conversation resumes)

SYBILL(on phone): Dammit! I just can't win with him. If it ain't one thing, it's another...don't be sending me off Jherma.

SABLE(putting flowers in vase): You always getting sent off.

SYBILL(on phone): I'll take care of that today. (She slams down phone.)

ASHA: Don't be rough-handling my phone, you don't pay the phone bill and you didn't buy the phone. So, get your own phone.

SYBILL(ignoring ASHA's statement): Peeve likes light-skinned girls. Jherma saw him under some girl's butt today.

SABLE: Don't worry about that, Peeve goes for all colors. He just wants to stick his gopher in somebody's hole.

ASHA: You just shut your mouth.

SYBILL(sarcastically): What's a gopher?

SABLE: Why don't you go ask somebody?

SYBILL(to ASHA): Mama, I'm going outside.

ASHA: You always wanna go outside, go, go, go.(She gets up and changes TV channel.) Ain't nothing outside but trouble.

SYBILL: I'm just gonna sit on the porch. (ASHA sits back down on the couch)

ASHA(putting her finger to her mouth): Shh, shh...they about to do the weather report.

SYBILL: It's not like you're going anywhere.

ASHA: I'll be...if you don't have the most flip mouth on this earth! (She leans back on the couch) You don't know where the hell I'm going.

SYBILL(curtly): Sorry, Mama. It just came out. (She gets up to exit)

ASHA(yelling behind SYBILL): You don't know where you're going either! (SYBILL slams door leading to her room) Don't be slamming MY doors in My face! You don't own a damn thing around here. (She lays back down on the couch and lights another cigarette) That mess made me miss the weather report. (SABLE looks at ASHA and shakes her head.)

SABLE: Is that all you need?

(LIGHTS DOWN)

SABLE'S VOICE: Maybe, if I turn myself inside out I'll see everything that's missing.

(Lights up in girls room. SABLE is reciting a poem accompanied with forceful mime in front of bureau mirror. She's barefoot. Sybill comes in mumbling bad phrases to herself.)

SABLE(still miming):...I've got five nose rings; a gold circle, a silver circle, a staaaar nefertitti, and a black moon...(she notices SYBILL) What's
your problem? (She plops down on SYBILL's bed out of breath.)

SYBILL(walking over to window): Will you please get your sweaty self
off my bed?

SABLE:I got cha.(She crawls off SYBILL's bed onto her own mattress.)
Humph! (She reaches under her mattress, removing a small notebook
and pen.) So what's your problem?

SYBILL: Don't worry about my problem. (She sits down on her bed and
rubs vigorously over her hair) Always in my business.

SABLE: I was just being a concerned sister.

SYBILL(abruptly): I don't need you to be concerned about me, you're not
my therapist or my mother.

SABLE: I know what I am.

SYBILL(innovating her voice to a nicer tone): While you're being yourself could you pick up some Ambi for me when you stop at the store?

SABLE: Ambi? That skin toning stuff? (She laughs.) What you up to
now?

SYBILL: Dammit! Stop asking me questions, either you'll get it for me or
you won't.

SABLE(persistently): Why? What do you need skin toner for? (She
chuckles to herself.) Your skin's already toned.

SYBILL: Nothing's funny! (She scoots off the bed and looks under it.) I'll
get it my damn self.

SABLE: That's it, honey! Take control of your life!

SYBILL: Where are my red shoes, Ms. Donahue?

SABLE: Which red shoes? You talking about those high-mountain ski
boots?

SYBILL: Yeah, those ski-boots that you wish you had.

SABLE: I don't wish for nothing, especially for any of your belongings. (She gestures toward the closet) They're in there, all of our shoes are organized in those boxes.

SYBILL: Don't touch my shoes.(She bends down in closet and begins to unorganize boxes.)

SABLE(flinging her notebook aside): What the hell are you trying to do? I spent at least two hours cleaning out that damn closet and you come busting in here messing stuff up!

SYBILL: No one asked you to do anything. Your always taking initiative for other folks. Leave me and mine alone. Don't make my bed, don't sweep around it, don't touch my clothes, don't touch my shoes! (She sits down on her bed and puts on shoes.)

SABLE: You'll never get another favor from me again. (She gets up off mattress and walks to mirror.) I've never met such an ungrateful person.

SYBILL: If you'd leave my stuff...

SABLE(interrupting): Drop it, sis.

SYBILL: Sometimes, you really make me sick. (She walks up behind SABLE)

SABLE: Don't touch me.

SYBILL(calmly): Just don't pull my number, Sable. (She walks toward door; looks back at Sable before she exits)

SABLE(to herself in front of mirror): Sister in rage and fury... (She presses the brush against her head) Like a violent tempest, she cracks against the breakers and the shaft-Eurus! (She mimes wind movement, moving around the room) Calm your fury down... (She rests against the window. There is a sudden loud knocking. Sable springs up.) Who's that?

(A sharp, deep voice answers back)

PEEVE: It's Peeve, come outside. I saw you in there gyrating. (SABLE pulls curtains back, they fall down. Peeve sticks his upper body in window

SABLE: What you doing peeping in my window, Peeve?

PEEVE: Just checking you out, cause I sho' want you to come out and talk to me for a minute.

SABLE(scrambling to fix curtains): Well, I can't come out right now. I'll get in trouble if people see me with you.

PEEVE: Who am I? (He pats his chest.) I'm just coming, trying to make a friend.

SABLE(frustrated): Come around the front.

(She places curtains back on wall, and rushes out the door)

(LIGHTS DOWN)

(Lights up in living room. ASHA is lying down on the couch in an awkward position. SABLE enters, acknowledges ASHA, then opens door leading to outside. Peeve is standing there smiling, wearing denim shorts, a white sleeveless t-shirt, and gym shoes.)

PEEVE: What's up? (He looks over her shoulders.) Ain't nobody here?

SABLE: Yeah.(She pulls him by the arm inside, then pushes him back out following behind.) What's on your mind?

(She crosses her arms and leans against the door)

PEEVE: Well, uh....I just peeped you dancing and all. I ain't never seen nobody do dat befoe. (He scratches his chin and stands with a slight slump)

SABLE:It's not really dancing, it's called mime...just adds...

PEEVE(interrupting): What you doing living at two-sixty-two Ronen then, Ms. Poetic Mimist? In a garden apartment?

SABLE: Forget you, Peeve. Everybody has to start from some form of a GA apartment and plug their way up.

PEEVE: Girl,...(he extends his arms over her shoulders)... you sho got a good head on your shoulders and you kinda cute. (He looks into her face, she looks aside)

SABLE: Thanks. (She moves away)

PEEVE(advancing towards her): I never got a good look at you befoe. (SABLE's eyes lock with his for a minute, then she turns to the door.)

SABLE: Well, I'll tell Sybill you came by to see her...

PEEVE(reaching into his back pocket and removing a box of cigarettes): I told you I ain't come by to see Sybill. (He lights cigarette.) I wanted to hear some of your poetry. (He smiles and touches her cheek, she looks away.)

SABLE: Bye, Peeve.

PEEVE: What, you gotta go?

SABLE(opening door): Obviously.

PEEVE: I'll be back. (He exits the stage. SABLE stands there watching him, then goes back inside.)

ASHA(yawning): Where you going?

SABLE: To my room.

ASHA: Could you pass me the matches? Where you coming from?

SABLE(sighing): You never question Sybill about her to's and fro's.

ASHA: Don't try to tell me what to do with my kids, just do what I say.

SABLE: I wasn't telling you what to do, I was just making a statement.

ASHA(raising her voice): Just pass me the damn matches!

SABLE(sternly): They're right in front of you.

ASHA(propping herself up on one arm): Hand me the matches now, Sable! (Sable stomps over, snatches matches off table.)

SABLE(extending hand): Here!

ASHA: You wait till I take them. (She puts cigarette in her mouth, then takes the matches.)

SABLE: Don't burn yourself. (Doorbell rings.) Whooh, saved by the bell.

ASHA(sitting up): Wonder who that is.

SABLE: Who else comes over here at three o'clock everyday ringing the doorbell like he's got a bad problem? (She walks to door muttering.) Must be Chuck's fat butt.

ASHA: What's wrong with you today, Sable? I've never heard you...

SABLE(opening door): I get provoked, too. I mean, day in and day out I'm constantly probed and nagged. I need a break.

 (CHUCK walks in wearing a grey pocketed t-shirt, badly wrinkled green shorts, and worn-out dress shoes. He shoves mail in SABLE's hand.)

SABLE: Well, come right on in Chuck!

(She slams door. CHUCK plants himself on the couch beside ASHA and gives her a fake brown flower.)

ASHA(to CHUCK): Did you bring my cigarettes?

CHUCK: You know I got em, babe. (He reaches into his shirt pocket and removes a box of cigarettes.) Sable, bring me some water!

ASHA(in a huff): How many times need I tell you that I DON'T smoke Newports? They're cancer sticks, and I know you don't want to kill me.

CHUCK: They didn't have anymore Benson & Hedges, Asha.

ASHA: You could've went to another store.

CHUCK: I could've made myself forget to bring you anything, always complaining about something. I ain't feel like walking to no other store...SABLE!!!

ASHA(slapping the box on the table): Well, I'll be damned. (She lights a cigarette. CHUCK gets up and changes TV channel.) Why you always gotta change the channel? That ain't your TV.

CHUCK: Now, don't start no bullshit! I works ten hours a day, buys your Benson & Hedges when they haves em at the sto', pays your bills, and takes you grocery shopping. Least I can do is watch a decent TV show.

(SABLE enters carrying a tall glass of ice water)

SABLE: Here you go, Chuck.

CHUCK(taking glass): You took so long, I almost don't want it. (He takes a sip)

SABLE: I hope you choke! (She bumps the couch as he sips, making him cough)

CHUCK: Watch yourself girl, you betta be careful.

SABLE: Next time get your own water.

CHUCK: I'll remember that the next time you ask me for something.

SABLE: I ain't never asked you for nothing!

ASHA: Sable, I don't know what your problem is today, but...

SABLE(interrupting): QUIET! (Turning her attention back to Chuck) I ain't never asked you to do nothing for me, and you've never done anything for me that I couldn't do for myself. (She holds up a letter and tosses the rest on the table.) All I have is this letter, a mattress, a few empty hangers, a notebook and myself. Which of those items have you given me?

CHUCK(chuckling to himself): You sho think you something, don't you?

SABLE: I...

ASHA(interrupting): Oh, shut up. We don't wanna know what you think you are. Where is the stuff I thought I told you to get from the store a long time ago?

SABLE(obviously filled to the brim in rage): I'm going now. (She exits)

LIGHTS DOWN

SABLE'S VOICE: I'm like white water in a deep dark well. (Lights come up in girl's room. SYBILL is applying cream to her face. There are several similar containers and liquids on her bed. SABLE enters.)

SABLE: Hey, Ambi. (She sits down on her mattress reading the front of the envelope.)

SYBILL: Hey, Gypsy woman.

SABLE: I had company while you were out.

SYBILL(nonchalantly): So?

SABLE: Well, since you don't care, never mind.

SYBILL(smudging cream around her eyes): Come on, tell me.

SABLE: Do you really want to know?

SYBILL: Not really.

SABLE: See, that's another thing about this family. No one gives a damn about what each other is up to. At least not the positive stuff, but I have a feeling you want to know real bad who came by to see me today. (She gets up and stands behind SYBILL looking in the mirror)

SYBILL: Get away before you make me mess up.

SABLE: Your already messed up! (She laughs and plops down on SYBILL's bed.) What's all this other stuff?

SYBILL: Get off my bed! Leave my stuff alone!

SABLE: I'm the one who made it this morning.

SYBILL: We straightened that out this morning...don't make my bed anymore.

SABLE(sitting down on her mattress): Peeve came by to see me today.

SYBILL(suspended): What?

SABLE: You heard me. While you were out wasting money on skin ton

184

ers and AMBI cream; trying to make your skin banana colored for Peeve, he wasn't even thinking about you.

SYBILL(She gets up and walks to window): Ummm... I see, he's gonna use you to get to me, and he doesn't even have to work that hard.

SABLE: I have never allowed myself to be used by anyone, and I won't be used by him.

SYBILL: You don't know the game, sweetheart.(She peeks out curtains, obviously spotting Peeve.) I'm an expert.

SABLE: Go for him then, I don't want him anyway.

SYBILL: Did he touch you?

SABLE: I told you I wouldn't allow myself to be used.

SYBILL: Did he touch you???

SABLE: Excuse me, salt water and potato chips, but that's none of your business. No, he didn't touch me.

SYBILL: I mean, because he could've had dirty hands. (She laughs and crosses her arms)

SABLE: Whatever. (She opens envelope and reads out loud.) Dear Black Box Poet, Congratulations! Your poem, along with ten others, has been selected out of 5000 entries to be published in the 1976-1977 edition of Black Box Poetry magazine.

SYBILL: Could you please read to yourself?

SABLE(excitedly): Mama! AAAAAH! (She jumps off mattress and scampers out the room.) Mama! They're gonna publish my poem!!!

SYBILL(to herself): So, the hell what. (She takes a paper towel and begins to wipe the cream off her face, A knock is heard at the window.) Yeah?

(She gets up and walks to window, pulls curtains completely back. Peeve is standing there smiling.)

PEEVE: Hey, Sybill. Where's Sable?

SYBILL: I'm not my sister's keeper, I don't know.

PEEVE: I didn't ask who you was keeping.

SYBILL: She's gone, now you be gone.

PEEVE: Man, Sybill why you so flip?

SYBILL: Instead of questioning my nature of being so flippant...

PEEVE(interrupting): Hold on, now...don't start transforming into Sable, using those big words and stuff. I mean, talk simple to me.

SYBILL: What do you mean, talk simple to you?

PEEVE: All those big words and long sentences make my brain strain. What's all that white stuff on your face?

SYBILL: Well, I sure as hell don't know how you expect to talk to my sister if words give you headaches.

PEEVE: It's the way she says em, she's so sweet.

SYBILL: You don't even know her...

PEEVE(interrupting): Just tell her I came by, OK? Yeah, and get that junk off your face. (He exits.)

LIGHTS DOWN

(Lights up in living room. Asha is smoking a cigarette. Chuck is twirling around the brown flower. Sable is speaking ardently to them.)

SABLE'S VOICE: I'll open up from a stem, into a petal, into a brown flower.

SABLE:...So it's gonna be published in the next edition.

ASHA: Be sure to share some of your earnings.

SABLE(angrily): Is that all you have to say? No congrats, no nothing?

I'm not sharing anything. Nobody helped me write that poem or even offered to be an audience when I practiced it.

ASHA: You expect everybody to stop what their doing, to listen to you all the time. No one owes you anything, Sable.

SABLE: I don't expect everybody to listen to me. However, from my family, I'd expect some recognition. (She sits down in the chair)

CHUCK: She's right, the family is supposed to stick together.

ASHA(snapping back): Oh, shut the hell up. When was the last time you went to a family reunion or made a trip to St. Louis to see your mother? When was the last time you made an effort to find your long lost son? When...

CHUCK(rubbing his head): We've all had our share of problems...my family wouldn't accept me because of mistakes I made in the past... just couldn't let go.

ASHA(sarcastically): Oh, aren't we all moved by your struggle. (She lights another cigarette) Back to you Sable, how much they gonna pay you?

SABLE: I don't know, a little for each copy.

CHUCK: When you make it big, Sable, don't forget about me.

ASHA: Now don't start filling her head up with that,"when you make it big" garbage. (Turning her attention to SABLE) Don't think you something cause a dis.

CHUCK(frustrated): Damn, Asha, give the child a little encouragement instead of knocking her all the time.

ASHA: That's my child, I know how to handle her...gotta make sure her head don't get too full.

CHUCK(to SABLE): Be sure to give me a copy. (He gets up and extends brown flower to SABLE)

SABLE(accepting flower): I won't, thank you. I mean, when I make it big I won't forget about you.

ASHA: Aaah, you just thinking big. Too big to be living here.

CHUCK(snapping): Just 'cause you 'gon be stuck in a garden apartment smoking Benson & Hedges for the rest of your life ALONE, 'cause I'm sho as hell leaving, don't mean she can't make it out! (He walks toward ASHA.)

ASHA(tapping her cigarette ashes on the floor): You ain't going no where.

CHUCK: Oh, yeah? I'm going back to Phoenix, and by the time I get there...

ASHA(interrupting): You'll still be lonely.(She stretches herself out on the couch.)

SABLE: You know Mama, everything doesn't have to be limited to right here in this room.

CHUCK(chuckling to himself as he walks toward the door): Yeah, baby...you sho got the right attitude. (He grasps the doorknob and looks back at SABLE.) That's one thing I gots to give you, attitude, you got it. (He exits. Sable walks to window, still grasping brown flower)

SABLE(to herself): Yeah, I got it.

BLACKOUT

An excerpt from
Daddy's Birthday
by Dolores Munoz

Daddy's Birthday, by Dolores Munoz. Fifteen-year-old Esperanza is embarrassed at being treated as if she were a little girl. She is also embarrassed by her mother's obsession, which is her dead husband, evidenced by a home shrine of flowers, a crucifix and a picture, to which her mother pays constant devotion. Miguel, Esperanza's brother, arrives home with a birthday cake. It becomes clear that the birthday celebration is for their dead father, a ritual that brother and sister find exceedingly strange, but are unwilling to stop. Amber, Esperanza's Anglo friend, arrives to take Esperanza out for the evening. Amber learns of the birthday party and urges Esperanza not to participate in the celebration for a ghost.

AMBER: (interrupting) ...let me finish. If somebody in my family started doing this stuff we'd have them admitted to a mental institution.

ESPERANZA: (interrupting) So you're saying my Mom is crazy.

(MAMI is at the door listening.)

AMBER: No, but what she's doing is.

ESPERANZA: But she's my Mom and I'm gonna have to accept it.

AMBER: What about you? How do you feel?

ESPERANZA; It doesn't matter, just as long as it makes Mami happy.

AMBER: You're always thinking about your Mom.... (stops...loses her point) This is insane... I'm gonna be in your room.

(AMBER sees MAMI and has an embarrassed look)

ESPERANZA: Hi Mami! (MAMI doesn't speak) Hi Mami!

(MIGUEL comes in)

MAMI (softly): Come on Miguel, help me set up.

(MIGUEL walks over to her and gives her a kiss on the cheek. ESPER-ANZA turns to her Mom.)

ESPERANZA: I'm sorry Mami. I had no right to do that.

MAMI(walks over to ESPERANZA and puts her hand on her shoulder): I forgive you mija. A mother always forgives her child no matter what.

ESPERANZA: I can't change you and I won't...

MAMI: I don't want you to try....

ESPERANZA(calmly): I'm sorry for trying to make you change.

(Long pause. Mother and daughter hug. Both are sobbing.)

MAMI: I really miss your father.

ESPERANZA: I do to. (She moves towards shrine) But, I can let go. Why can't you.

MAMI(starts to tear): I don't know... I still think he's here and he knows that I can cope with anything. When your father died I was alone. I had to raise both you and your brother by myself. I was so scared. (she stares at shrine) That strong front was for you kids. I felt like a lost puppy. The only thing that kept me going was your father. It's like I was able to see him and talk to him. All I had to do was reach out my hand and he would touch it and guide me. He was the one who took care of everything and well, alone, I didn't know what to do.

ESPERANZA: I had no idea.

MAMI: No one did. I never told anybody how I felt. I would just wake up, go to work, and clean those rich ladies' houses to put food in your mouths...but sometimes when your brother went to bed, I would stay up and cry myself to sleep. (long pause)

ESPERANZA: (walks toward her mom and hugs her) I'm so sorry Mami. (MAMI is in a daze)

MAMI: I know I should stop and move on.

ESPERANZA: (interrupts) You don't have to Mami (cries) if that makes you happy.

MIGUEL: (beginning to tear) I love you just the way you are.

ESPERANZA: Don't worry Mom, I'm gonna stay for the party.

MAMI: (staring at the shrine) Well, I do want to change that's it. I'm freeing myself from him ...you are right Esperanza, I can't keep living a fantasy. I love your father, but I have to move on.   (ESPERANZA puts her arm around her mom and they both look at the shrine. She gestures to MIGUEL) Go get me a box from the closet. Esperanza, help me. (MAMI starts to take the shrine apart. ESPERANZA stares at her and begins to help. MIGUEL walks in and starts to put the stuff in the box)

MIGUEL: Are you sure you want to do this?

MAMI: Positive. I need to let go (MAMI picks up box and exits)

ESPERANZA: Did I start all this?

MIGUEL: You sure did...I always told you to be careful for what you wish for....

ESPERANZA: ...cuz you might get it! (they both chuckle) I can't believe Mami is doing this.

MIGUEL: Me either.

ESPERANZA: What do you think she's gonna do now?

MIGUEL: I don't know...I hope she doesn't buy a motorcycle...

ESPERANZA: Could you imagine that! (pause) Are we still gonna have the party.

MIGUEL: I don't know... maybe she'll throw the cake away.

ESPERANZA: I hope not, it looks good. (pause) Man, Mami has had it really hard; first her mother died when she was five years old, and then Papi...I'd die if that happened to me.

MIGUEL: I thought I had it hard when Papi died...poor mom.

ESPERANZA: (begins to sob) Why couldn't this happen to somebody else. Mami is the nicest person in the world...that's just not fair.

MIGUEL: Nothing's fair...that's just how things work (comforts ESPERANZA)

ESPERANZA: (still crying) It sucks. (Long pause)

MIGUEL: (gets up and looks out exit) I wonder what Mom is doing?

ESPERANZA: (a few tears but not crying) She's probably throwing away everything that reminds her of Papi.

MIGUEL: I hope not...I don't want to forget him.

ESPERANZA: Neither do I.

MIGUEL: But Mom does.

ESPERANZA: Now the tables are turning...

MIGUEL: For you...I never really minded Mom. I kind of liked it.

ESPERANZA: I feel bad now... I feel like I took Mami's sense of security away.

MIGUEL: Don't feel bad...Mami is an adult. She decided this all on her own.

ESPERANZA: (crying) I know but...(Mami enters. They stop. They walk towards her.)

MIGUEL: (to ESPERANZA) Is everything okay? (ESPERANZA wipes her eyes with her sleeves. MIGUEL walks over to MAMI and bends down to her face.) Are you okay?

MAMI: Si Mejo, everything is fine.

MIGUEL: Good, Do you want to start.

MAMI: Sure, pass me the knife and some forks, I'll get the candles and the napkins, Esperanza take the cake out of the box. (ESPERANZA is quiet as AMBER walks in.)

AMBER: Are you still gonna go with me? (ESPERANZA doesn't answer) (hesitantly) Esperanza are you? (MAMI and MIGUEL are on each side of ESPERANZA DR ...AMBER is UL)

MAMI: Answer her Meja.

ESPERANZA: No, I'm gonna stay for the party.

AMBER: But he's dead.

ESPERANZA: Only to you.

AMBER: This is weird...I'm leaving... I'll see you at school.

ESPERANZA: Alright... (yells) Amber, are you sure you don't want to stay?

AMBER: No thanks (steps out the door but comes back in quickly) Happy Birthday wherever you are. (AMBER leaves. ESPERANZA joins the party.)

ESPERANZA: Let's sing.

MIGUEL: In Spanish or English.

ESPERANZA: How about both? (MAMI is smiling they all turn toward cake, light candles and they begin to sing in English.)

CURTAIN

An excerpt from

Mommy Wants a Pony
(a.k.a. "Sing Praise: Mother and Child")

by Abbie Kruse

Mommy Wants A Pony, by Abbie Kruse. Naomi and her boyfriend Trevor lie on a rooftop, having tagged some walls with red paint. Without getting specific, they plan an event for later that evening. Naomi goes home and transforms herself from street-talking girl to the perfect daughter, happily conversing with her mother, Reba. Trevor phones, and Naomi says they must meet at a friend's house for "the event." Gradually, the mother/daughter conversation darkens, turning into Naomi's past delinquency and her choice of "loser" friends. Naomi accuses Reba of being a mother when it is convenient.

NAOMI: I feel good. I feel damn good. (she gets up, stretches, and turns a cartwheel. she poses a victorious pose, as if presenting herself to the world)

TREVOR: Girl, sit down. You won't feel so good when some cop shags us down and takes your markers.

NAOMI: True dat, true dat. (she sits back down, her legs over TREVOR's lap, perpendicular to him) How do you feel?

TREVOR: Nice. Mellow. Happy. I feel like I could tag the moon. (gestures with a spray can. pause.) If it was night. (they laugh)

NAOMI: What would you write?

TREVOR: My life story. In three words.

NAOMI: Only three?

TREVOR: That's all I need.

NAOMI: What three words?

TREVOR: (laughs, says slowly, counting on his fingers) Messed up kid.

My head feels really big.

NAOMI: (laughing) That's so dope, mine does too. At least it doesn't hurt.

TREVOR: Mmmmm, I'm coming down very gently. It's nice.

NAOMI: (rocks her head side to side) I think I need a nap. And something to drink. And a big comfy chair. And some funky music. And a black candle. And a shower. Not necessarily in that order.

TREVOR: Showers are for the weak. We are strong. Rrrr. See us stomp about on rooftops, scrawling our names on brick and stone. We are immortalized in red paint. We are invincible.

NAOMI: (rubs her head against his neck) We are invincible and greasy, my brotha.

TREVOR: But we do it so well, my sista.

NAOMI: I like being good at what I do.

TREVOR: You get high really well. And you give the best hugs. (hugs her) And you carry grease with a certain grace.

NAOMI: (laughs) Thanks, baby.

TREVOR: Don't mention it. (pause)

NAOMI: Are you going home with me?

TREVOR: No, I've got to go to my home and feed my little brothers. My parents have no critical thinking skills, yo. My brothers can stay home alone all day, but they can't use the stove to make themselves a can of soup. Does that make sense?

NAOMI: No, of course not. When do your folks ever make sense? My ma is the same way.

TREVOR: (looks at her lovingly and hugs her close, presses his forehead to hers) I'll be over later.

NAOMI: (smiles and kisses his nose) Good. (pulls back a bit and looks down) I love you.

TREVOR: I love you. Are you nervous?

NAOMI: No, I want to. I really want to.

TREVOR: It's weird, though, isn't it? Personally, I'm scared out of my drug fried mind. (pause)

NAOMI: I'm bout to be up. I'ma go home and take a shower and pine for you.

TREVOR: I'll be over about 7. Is that okay? Too late?

NAOMI: Naw, you can come over whenever you're done at home. Take care of your brothers.

(NAOMI gets up into a crouch and looks over the top of the wall. TREVOR follows suit.)

TREVOR: I don't see anybody.

NAOMI: Let's go.

(She starts to stand up, but he pulls her down and gives her a quick kiss. They smile at each other for a moment, then together they swing a leg over the wall and slide down until only their fingers and hands are visible on the front edge. They pause for a moment, then their hands and fingers disappear. The lights fade to black on the platform and come up on the kitchen. REBA sits at kitchen table facing audience. On the table is an ashtray complete with a burning cigarette, a glass of iced tea, and two piles of mail, opened and unopened. REBA drags on the cigarette, studies a piece of mail, drinks some tea, shakes her head to herself. We hear keys unlocking a door. REBA takes a last drag, stubs the butt out slowly, stands up, throws the accumulated ash and butts away, we hear running water as she washes the ashtray. Naomi enters, eyes on the floor, singing, as REBA washes. Naomi looks up, surprised.)

NAOMI:(recovering) Hey, mama! What's goin' down?

REBA:(over her shoulder) Hey, kid. Nothing is going on. I just started opening the ever-loving bills.

NAOMI: Fun.(kisses REBA's cheek) You're certainly home early. It's only (checks watch) five o'clock.

REBA: Well, my work was practically done, so I took off early. Perks of a supervisor position.

NAOMI:(smiling) Cool. Abusing your power. (NAOMI puts her backpack on the table and hangs her jacket on the back of the chair previously occupied by REBA)

REBA: What little power I have.

NAOMI: What happened today in the exciting world of printing and publishing, may I ask? NAOMI grabs an apple from a basket on the counter)

REBA: You may. (pause)

NAOMI: Okay, so what happened?

REBA:(smiling) Nothing. It was the same today as it has been every day of every week for the past four years. Except, of course, for the day that Mrs. Sewell collapsed with a heart attack. And the day Ms. Braun dropped her potted plant out of the window- just to see it fall- and when we called her doctor we found out she was supposed to be taking 25mg of Lithium a day. Hrumph. Outpatients. And...well, no, that's it. Today was perfectly routine and awfully boring. Even the periodic gurgling of the water cooler has ceased to break up the monotony. (thoughtful and still for a moment) I think I need a change.

NAOMI:(looking up from the mail she has been rifling through and swallowing a mouthful of apple) You always say that.

REBA: I know. But this time I mean it.

NAOMI: You always say that, too.

REBA:(ignoring her) I did get stopped by two trains on the way home today. I've decided to interpret it as a bad omen. Death, disease, something horrible.

NAOMI: My throat does feel kinda scratchy.

REBA: That's it, then.

NAOMI:(looking at a piece of mail) Dad sent a check.

REBA:(looking) Finally. You know, even though he doesn't come to see you or your sister, he could at lease send your baby payments on time. (pause)

NAOMI: Where is the peanut of the house?

REBA: Your younger sister is staying with your grandmother until Wednesday next.

NAOMI: She's been there all summer. (looks absently into space)

REBA: I know, but Gram does love to have her there. Do you remember when you spent every free moment of your summers with Grandma? We couldn't pry you away from her with a crowbar and high-tension steel cable. As a matter of fact, at one point you spent so much time in her cozy abode that you began to feel guilty about neglecting me.

NAOMI:(sad) I remember. (bravado) I was such a foolish child. I should have savored that time. (teasing smile to REBA)

REBA:(smiles back) I found something you made for me that was produced by childish guilt. (pulls a paper from the bottom of the stack of opened mail) A beautiful...impressionist depiction of... (turns it over, top to bottom)

NAOMI:(without looking) A horse.

REBA: I loved it. I still do. (melodramatic) It reminds me that there was a time when you still loved me!

NAOMI:(laughs. Ends with a nervous cough) (pause)

NAOMI: Ask me about my day. (gets up, crosses to counter)

REBA: What should I ask?

NAOMI:(pouring a drink) Ask me how it went.

REBA: How did your day go, darling?

NAOMI: It went very well, thank you. (sits in same seat) Like clockwork. The sun rose, followed a traditional arc across the sky, and is now dipping down- ready to plunge back below the horizon. Or, I should say, the EARTH revolved around its axis, blahblahblah. (pause, drink) Work was typical. Afterward I played a smashing game of death Frisbee in the park with Paul and Liz and Boy.

REBA: (eyebrow raised) Death Frisbee?

NAOMI: Yes. Very fast and very dangerous. In a public area, you whip a saucer-shaped piece of stiff plastic from person to person in a random manner. The danger of hitting passersby is enormous. So is the danger of losing the Frisbee in the furious throw and catch rhythm of the game.

REBA: Foreshadowing that this is precisely what happened to you?

NAOMI: Precisely. Paul made a particularly fast and dangerous and sadly miscalculated throw that landed the hapless Frisbee on the roof of the park fieldhouse near which we were playing.

REBA: Really?

NAOMI: Truly.

REBA: Extraordinary.

NAOMI: Devastating. Our game stopped. The only solution we could devise was to climb up on the roof of the fieldhouse and retrieve our lost toy. As Boy and Paul were boosting Liz up onto a ledge, a blue-clad sil-ver-badged policeman walked out of the front doors of the fieldhouse. Picture it: Liz halfway up the building, frozen to the stone, and we hunched over guiltily under her. "The Man" staring at us, confused.

REBA: It's vivid.

NAOMI: I'm transfixed just listening to myself. Anyway, "The Man" snapped out of his bovine confusion and preoccupation with young day camp boys' bare legs to reveal the startling fact that we weren't supposed to be climbing on the building. We pleaded our case to him with enough sincerity and earnest looks to fill a bushel basket, but to no avail. He was unmoved. He searched Paul and Boy, the enjoyment obvious on his face, and found a thick red paint-marker in Paul's bag. From this evi-dence he wrongly deduced that Paul was a tagger. Long story short, we were escorted out of the park, Paul's art marker was confiscated, and we never got our Frisbee back.

REBA:(laughs) I'd clap, but I'd ash all over the floor. Your friends really make me laugh, Naomi. Is your room clean?

NAOMI:(stretches as REBA starts to laugh, notices her watch and jumps up) It's late. I have to make a call.

(Naomi crosses stage left to a phone behind a partition immediately adjacent to the kitchen. She takes the phone off the hook and dials.)

NAOMI: Yo baby. (pause) Nothin, you? (pause) Listen, uh, I think we're gonna have to call it off. We can't do it at my house, anyway. (pause) My ma's home. (pause) I don't know, she just took off work early and now she's home and she's...doin dishes and stuff. (pause) I know, I'm sorry. I really wanted to. Hey, you wanna do it a little later? (pause) I was thinkin Boy's house. They're on vacation and he gave me a key a week ago for emergencies. (pause) I'm tellin you, she is never home this early. It's a freak coincidence, never happened in a million years. I'll ask her if I can go out. She's got to say yes. (pause) Don't worry, I'll call you back in a few minutes and I'll see you tonight. (pause) Bye, sweetie. Bye. (hangs up) (Naomi re-enters kitchen. Sits down at table and takes a drink. Puts her feet up on the table.)

REBA:(over her shoulder from the counter where she is mixing something in a pitcher) Put your feet on the floor.

(Naomi does so and clears her throat)

REBA: Have you...planned something for this evening, my little social butterfly?

NAOMI: Maybe. Perhaps. I've been invited to venture out into the wondrous world of Boy's house.

REBA: Naomi, is your room clean?

NAOMI: Spotlessly so. I even went so far as to dust the tiny ceramic animals our relatives are so persistent in foisting upon me.

REBA: What about the bathroom? I did tell you to pay some attention to it, didn't I?

NAOMI: Yes, you did. And yes, I did. It is quite clean.

REBA: The back room has been vacuumed?

NAOMI: Yeah.

REBA: You moved everything and did the edging?

NAOMI: Ma, everything is done. (pause) Can I go? (pause, REBA is silent) It's just to Boy's house with Liz and Paul and maybe Trevor. We're going to watch a movie, listen to some muzak, eat Boy's food and I'll be home by 11:30. I've even got a ride.

REBA: I don't know. You've been out a lot this week. It is the fashion, in some circles, to spend a quiet evening at home. No, I think it's best you stay in and take a break from partying tonight.

NAOMI: Now, I haven't been out a lot this week, ma. Only twice.

REBA: (lightly) Oh, you've been out more than that.

NAOMI: No, only twice. (pause)

REBA: I don't want you to go out.

NAOMI: (slowly) Why? Where's the logic?

REBA: Where's your respect? I said no. What's wrong with you today?

NAOMI: Nothing! (calming) Nothing. I'm just...I really wanted to go out with my friends.

REBA: You saw them all day today. And...(sadly) I don't know if I like your friends.

NAOMI: What?!

REBA: (matter-of-factly) They leave a mess whenever they come over.

NAOMI: We clean it up.

REBA: They use language I don't like you to be around.

NAOMI: Oh, COME ON...

REBA:(getting angry) They get you in trouble, which isn't something you need help with...

NAOMI:(eyes closed, vocally tops REBA) Please don't go there. (pause) It's painful ancient history that I don't want dredged up every time you need to have something against me.

REBA: No, I think it needs to be brought up. You forget things so easily. Let me refresh your memory. Let's talk about a 27 year old man and a 15 year old girl caught together in a car by the police doing God knows what when she told her mother she was going to be at the library. Do you want to talk about that?

NAOMI:(hand over eyes) That was two years ago, ma.

REBA: Well then what about the 17 year old girl who gets on a bus to go to school, but ends up on Belmont and Halsted shopping when she's supposed to be in 3rd period English? Or the 17 year old girl who, while grounded for that, decides to sneak out and spend all night running around with her friends because her mother wasn't home? (silence) Well?

NAOMI: What can I say to that? I served my time, I paid for my crimes. I never objected to my punishments, did I?

REBA: No. But the fact remains, you've abused my trust countless times in the past. It hurts to know your daughter doesn't respect you and lies to your face constantly. The people you call "friends" have been very bad influences on you.

NAOMI:(softly) They are friends. Real friends.

REBA: They're a bunch of zeroes and they're going nowhere fast. They're also encouraging you to break my laws and compromise your morals, if you have any left to compromise.

NAOMI: You don't know what you're saying. You really don't know what you're insinuating.

REBA: We won't even get into your moral standing. What about the stunt you pulled today? Playing a dangerous game and getting in trouble with the police are the reasons I'm supposed to trust you now? I should ground you for going to the park without permission. Your past is enough reason to be hard on you.

NAOMI:(is silent for a moment, shaking her head, confused) I came home today and talked to you like a friend because that's how you acted. Now you're my personal dictator. Am I the only one here who thought about what just came out of your mouth? How can you justify anything you've said? Every sentence you speak is a contradiction of yourself. Go ahead- be strict. But don't be manic like you are now. I wish you'd be my mother all the time and not just when the mood strikes you. I can't handle the leaps you make between mother and friend. (looks away, arms folded)

REBA: What about you? Sometimes you're cheerful and happy, sometimes you're quiet and depressed. We all have our moods. (puts her hands on NAOMI's shoulders)

NAOMI: Sure we all have changes in our moods. But, if you'll notice, my mood changes don't involve damaging your peace of mind. I don't blow up at you for any little thing. I don't pretend to be your friend one minute and then stab you in the back the next.

REBA:(ignoring her totally) I'm only human. This is how people are. Complex. We have mood swings. We're human. And humans do unexplainable, inscrutable things. Like buying season Cubs tickets.

NAOMI:(gets up and shrugs off REBA's hands) Stop it! This isn't a game! It's real. Humanity is not defined by mood swings. Humans are often cruel, but that's not an excusable reason to be cruel, just because you're human. And you are being cruel....

REBA: Stop it, Naomi, I was trying to end this. Look, you have this vision of motherhood that is totally unrealistic. I'm a real person, just like you're a real person. People aren't perfect. You don't expect yourself to be perfect and calm and even-tempered all the time, do you? You give yourself a little leeway when it comes to your emotions, don't you? Why can't you give me the same allowances? You're making my head ache.

NAOMI:(cold) I wasn't done. You are being cruel (her voice rises above REBA's protests) and I'm tired of it. Okay, I'm a real person, but you don't treat people this way. It's wrong.

(REBA storms out)

NAOMI: (quietly) I'm tired of keeping quiet while you're blatantly unfair and too, too human. (her voice gets louder to follow REBA) Do I ever talk back? Think about it. NO. The answer is no. I never say a word when you yell or when you're mean, so I think I've earned this. I can't stay quiet now. This is something that's been inside of me for a long time. (rifles through her bag) I need to tell you and you need to hear it.

REBA: (yells from off) I don't need to hear anything! I told you I don't want to continue this conversation!

NAOMI: (quieter, but still loud enough to be heard by REBA) I'm sorry, ma. I need to read this to you. (flips through the notebook she's pulled out of her bag) I wrote a letter to no one about you. Maybe it was to you. It's how I feel.

REBA: (appears behind NAOMI) You wrote about me?

NAOMI: (sits down at table on SL side) About you. Listen. (reads from notebook) "If this was a real relationship and you treated me this way, we'd have no relationship. I'd hate you. If I were a real person to you, you wouldn't treat me this way. You wouldn't be around to do it. (pause) I'd have told you to take off long ago...."

REBA: Naomi! Don't you dare use that type of language!

NAOMI: Listen! Calm down and listen! This is a part of me and that was how I felt at the time. This is the truth. "Today I saw the point at which I should have said those two biting words. I saw something that made me remember a time when I was just a little kid, younger than I am now, when you said something to me."

REBA: (absently, to no one, not looking at Naomi or listening) You were a dancer and a water baby. You smothered me with kisses.

(the lights fade to black, two spotlights remain on the actors)

NAOMI: (to herself) I remember... (reading again) "I don't remember what happened, why you were mad, I don't remember you. But I can see myself from outside myself stepping back in shock as you said, 'JUST GET WAY FROM ME' when I tried to hug you. You said that and I cried."

REBA: I remember you running around naked in a pair of oversized sun glasses. I couldn't keep clothes on you.

NAOMI: Ten minutes later you spoke to me as if nothing had happened and I was grateful because my mommy let me put my arms around her again. I was too grateful to question the rightness of it. I forgot it. Until the next time.

REBA: You would hug me and tell me I was your best friend. I wanted it to be true.

NAOMI: You did it so much, it seems. Scream and push me away one minute and talk to me calmly the next. 'Naomi, you are such a wonderful person. I wish I were more like you. What's wrong with you?'

REBA: You were such a good kid. You never complained, you always ate your vegetables, and you were kind to animals. I told you I was waiting for you to do something really bad. I was joking. But then you did.

NAOMI: It got to where I didn't even feel it anymore. 'JUST GET AWAY FROM ME' didn't make me cry anymore. You didn't have to say it anymore because I didn't try to wrap my arms around you and tell you not to be mad anymore. I don't need your forgiveness now, and I'm not grateful when I get it.

REBA: You lied. You lied and told me he was just an older friend, you lied and told me it was over when I found out your first lie, you lied and told me what I wanted to hear and I wanted to believe you.

NAOMI: I wanted to tell you how I felt, but I couldn't. I was too overcome by what I saw you do to my 11 year old sister to say what I wanted to say. She forgot to clean your birdcage. Your birdcage. So you bared your teeth at her like some dog and she ran to her room to cry. When she came back it was straight faced and repentant. She tried to help you put away some groceries and bumped you in the process. You were squatting in front of the refrigerator, obsessively cleaning what need not be cleaned, bitching under your breath at the world for dealing you this bad hand, these bad kids, this bad life. She apologized to you and put her hand on the back of your head. In the moment you looked up at her and hesitated, when you could have said, 'It's okay', you said 'JUST GET AWAY FROM ME, DON'T TOUCH ME!' That's when she should have said what I should have said years ago.

REBA: You were closed to me. You weren't my best friend of picture drawing tradition anymore. Your face was unreadable. You are still an artist of sorts, but now your craft is deception, and not horse-drawing.

NAOMI:(speaking, not reading) You know why I made that horse for you, ma? I wanted you to say I was worth something and that I wasn't just a burden that wouldn't let you get a job. She needs it now. She needs you. Wait 'til she starts mailing you pictures from grandma's house.

REBA: You had become proficient at what's called the straight-faced lie. And you did it more than once.

NAOMI:(louder, reading again) 'Just get away from me you vile disgust-ing thing, you weight, you burden.' This rung in my ears, though you never said it out loud. 'If it weren't for you I could have had a better life. Just get away from me, don't put your revolting little hands anywhere near me.' It's not just me anymore. You're doing it again, to my little sister.

REBA:(louder) You broke my trust, and hurt me more than you'll ever know. I couldn't sleep nights worrying that you didn't love me any-more...

NAOMI: ...and I worried you had never loved me...

REBA: ...knowing what you hadn't realized, that I needed your approval as much as you needed mine.

(lights up slowly)

NAOMI:(turns in her chair so that their backs are to each other) I was a little dancer, wasn't I?

REBA: Yes. But now you're... someone else. I don't sleep nights worry-ing that you don't love me...and that you're out somewhere loving someone else. Trevor... (REBA trails off)

NAOMI: Say it! Say what you mean! Stop hinting and insinuating things. I can't stand when you do that.

REBA: I can't accept that you've...(trails off again)

NAOMI: HAD SEX? I haven't! You never asked me, though, did you? You just assumed.

REBA:(sarcastic) You haven't. (pause, then sincere) You haven't?

NAOMI:(looks over her shoulder) No.

REBA:(thinks) Why not?

(silence)

NAOMI:(shrugs) I was going to....tonight.

REBA: That's why you were so...

NAOMI: Yeah. That's why I was...whatever.

REBA: Oh. (she turns to face NAOMI, whose back is actually still to her.)

NAOMI: I only lied to you because I knew you'd say no if I told you the truth. (turns to look at REBA) But then you started calling me a liar and I felt bad because I don't lie nearly as much as you think I do and I wanted to tell you the truth. About tonight. About everything. (holds up horse picture)

REBA:(looking away, out into space. Talks as much to herself as to NAOMI) You aren't a little girl anymore. You have to make your own decisions about...things. I can't hold you forever. Next year you're going to college. I won't be able to say no anymore. I've been afraid of that for a while. (sigh. looks at NAOMI now) This is when you're sup-posed to be growing up, isn't it? I have to accept it, don't I?

NAOMI: Yeah. Yes. But who are you? Are you saying that as my friend or as my mother? I expected you to be mad...

REBA: I don't know. I'm your mother. I'm your friend. I don't know. (to herself) Why aren't I mad. (pause) Maybe I don't care. Maybe I should-n't care. (tired. sits down opposite NAOMI) Maybe I've been wrong to care at all these past few years. You're older than I thought you were.

NAOMI: Is this another one of your guilt trips or...(looks closely at REBA) You really mean it. Don't you? (pause. then quietly, to her hands on the table) You don't care. What do you...but...but I want you to care. I still want you to care... (trails off a she looks up into REBA's face again)

REBA:(smiling softly) You can't let go either, can you? (pause) You know how I feel, but in reverse. And you have my gift for contradiction. You want to be free, but you still want me. It's painfully ironic, isn't it? (long pause)

NAOMI:(speaking softly, looking down) Do we still need each other or are we just messed up? (NAOMI looks up slowly until her eyes meet REBA's. They stare at each other for a long time.)

REBA:(clears her throat) Dinner.

NAOMI:(annoyed) What?

REBA: I've got to do something about dinner.

NAOMI:(turning away again) I'm not hungry.

REBA: Neither am I. (attempting to return to glib banter) We really should eat something anyway.

NAOMI: You're probably right.

REBA: Of course I'm right. But I don't feel like cooking anything. Any suggestions?

NAOMI:(trying to recover) We could eat leftover chicken and corn. (sadly) That would sustain us this day so that we might live another.

REBA: Brilliant. (trying to smile) Would you mind, um, pulling it out of the refrigerator and warming it to edible temperature in the blasted contraption?

NAOMI:(heavily) The microwave?

REBA: Yes.

NAOMI: Yeah. (to herself) So we're back to the game again. It hurts. I can't tell her everything. Ever. I don't want to play anymore.

REBA: I'm going to change into something a little less corporate... and call your sister.

(REBA looks at NAOMI for a reaction. She doesn't get one. Exits. NAOMI pulls something out of the fridge and puts it on the counter. Sits again- facing audience. She stares at her notebook for a moment, then pushes it aside. She picks up the horse picture and stares at it. Shakes her head to herself.)

(curtain down)

An excerpt from
WINE WITH DINNER
by Nicole Conforti

Wine With Dinner, by Nicole Conforti. Naima nervously prepares dinner for her mother and herself. When mother arrives home, there is talk of her commission on the sale of a house, which will enable them to take a vacation. We learn that Naima's father recently ran off with another woman. Over dinner (the mother's food accompanied by several glasses of wine), Naima plans for her impending graduation from high school. Her mother becomes increasingly defensive about the drinking issue, missing the irony of her looking for a bottle of vodka even as she protests she does not have a problem.

(MOTHER enters)

MOTHER: NAIMA? I'm home

NAIMA: I'm in the kitchen. I just finished dinner (MOTHER goes in the kitchen and gives NAIMA a kiss hello. Then she goes and hangs her jacket over the chair NAIMA will sit in during dinner) How was work?

MOTHER: It was fine, thanks

NAIMA: So?

MOTHER: So, what?

NAIMA: (anxious) Come on, tell me

MOTHER: (laughingly) Tell you what?

NAIMA: Did you sell the house?

MOTHER: (calmly, brushing it off) Yeah.

NAIMA: (happy) Oh my god!

MOTHER: I got a $5,000 commission

NAIMA: So does that mean we can go out to New York to Grandma and Grandpa's for the summer?

MOTHER: Possibly. All your cousins are supposed to go right?

NAIMA: Yeah

MOTHER: I'll call some of your aunts and uncles tonight. Gosh. I can't wait to see everyone. It's been almost 6 months.

NAIMA: Oh, by the way, Grandma Felicia called today.

MOTHER: (questioning) Why?

NAIMA: She asked me to go out there for the summer...

(MOTHER interrupts)

MOTHER: You told her you were spending it with your real family, my family right?

NAIMA: Yeah... so she asked me if winter break was o.k., and I said I didn't know, but I want to. I haven't seen Dad in so long.

MOTHER: You mean since he left almost a year and a half now. How can you want to see him after he walked out of your life for that sleazy little tramp?

NAIMA: And yours. Plus I miss him. Please? At least think about it before saying no.

MOTHER: I didn't plan on saying no, but I do have to think about it. So how was school?

NAIMA: Fine. We just practiced for graduation.

MOTHER: Did you get all of the tickets I ordered?

NAIMA: Yeah.

MOTHER: Good. I might need extra.

NAIMA: God. At this rate, my family is just going to fill up the whole stadium.

(MOTHER pulls wine out of fridge, and sets it on the table)

NAIMA: Oh, and I also need some more summer clothes.

MOTHER: So what are you saying? You want me to buy them for you. To what do I owe the honor?

NAIMA: Well, if you insist.

MOTHER: Ha, ha. Very funny. You have your own job.

NAIMA: That pays like crap.

MOTHER: So find another one. Better yet; just get a second one.

NAIMA: With graduation right around the corner, and summer coming up, I'll never get a job. All of the college kids get the good jobs, and I'm not about to work at Burger King.

MOTHER: What's wrong with Burger King? A job is a job. You know when I was your age, I worked in your uncle Freddie's barn. He only paid me 75 cents an hour. And do you know the kind of work I was doing? It wasn't pretty. Compared to my job, do you know how easy you have it?

NAIMA: But Mother, this is Burger King we are talking about. Gross greasy, processed food.

MOTHER: No one said you had to eat it.

NAIMA: But I have to look at it, and smell it.

MOTHER: Beggars can't be choosers, and choosers can't be beggars.

NAIMA: Fine. I'll think about it. I highly doubt that I'm going to get another job because like I said, summer is just around the corner, and only the college kids get the good jobs.

MOTHER: Just don't expect to make $10.00 an hour.

NAIMA: I know that. So, are you going to take me shopping?

MOTHER: Just remember, I'll tell you like I tell you every time we go out shopping, if I don't like it, you can't get it.

NAIMA: But they are my clothes, and I have to wear them.

MOTHER: (shrugs her shoulders) So what's your point?

NAIMA: Why are you being so difficult, Mother?

(They go and sit down to eat. NAIMA sits in the chair with her MOTHERS coat hanging on the back of it.)

MOTHER: Let's just talk about this later. I just want to eat a nice quiet dinner.

NAIMA: Fine. (there is a pause. NAIMA smells something funny. She is not quite sure what it is. She finally smells her moms coat hanging on the back of her chair.)

MOTHER: Pass me a napkin, sweetheart.

NAIMA: Mom, why does your jacket smell of really heavy cigarette smoke?

MOTHER: Because I stopped out after work.

NAIMA: Really? Where?

MOTHER: Don't worry about it.

NAIMA: I am worried. Where did you go?

MOTHER: (with some hesitation) Out.

NAIMA: (getting mad) Out where?

MOTHER: (takes a bite, and when she is done chewing, she answers NAIMA's question.) I just went out for a couple of drinks with some friends. That's all. See, no big deal.

NAIMA: (mumbling) As usual.

MOTHER: What?

NAIMA: Nothing.

MOTHER: Go ahead, say it. Say it out loud.

NAIMA: What?

MOTHER: What you just said.

NAIMA: I don't remember.

MOTHER: Stop acting like you're a three year old.

(MOTHER pours a glass of wine.)

NAIMA: So that's why you were late coming home today. I should have known. I never can expect you to come home straight home from work, can I?

MOTHER: Oh, stop it already. I'm not in the mood to fight with you today, so just let it go.

NAIMA: NO!

MOTHER: (angry) What? Don't you ever, ever tell me no in my house ever again. Do you understand that young lady? (pause)   Answer me.

NAIMA: (softly) Yes.

MOTHER: What?

NAIMA: (loudly) YES, I heard you

(As they fight, NAIMA keeps eyeing the bottle of wine, and MOTHER notices.)

MOTHER: If you have a problem, I suggest you go and eat somewhere else. (NAIMA gets up with her plate.) Where do you think you're going? (NAIMA just looks at her and doesn't say anything.) I asked you a question, now answer me. Where are you going?

NAIMA: You said if I had a problem to go and eat somewhere else. Now tell me, what the hell does it look like I'm doing.

MOTHER: Stop being such a smart-ass, and sit down.

NAIMA: (angrily) You said I should go and eat somewhere else. And what if I feel like standing?

MOTHER: (unimpressed) Sit down.

NAIMA: (threatening) No

MOTHER: (exhausted) I just want a peaceful dinner. I've had a hard day.

NAIMA: Of what. Drinking?

(MOTHER glares at her)

MOTHER: Could you get me some orange juice? I need a drink.

NAIMA: I think you've had enough.

MOTHER: (getting mad) Don't tell me when I've had enough. I can tell. And I want you to go and get some orange juice in a glass for me now, please. (NAIMA doesn't move) I'm your mother. You have to listen to me.

NAIMA: Well you don't act like it.

MOTHER: What is your problem?

NAIMA: Do you honestly want to know?

MOTHER: (excitedly) Yes!

(NAIMA goes to sit back down. She is not as upset anymore.)

NAIMA: It's everything. This house, your rules, being alone, work, school...you.

MOTHER: You're just upset because graduation is right around the corner, and you're nervous.

NAIMA: No mom, it's not graduation. Weren't you listening to me?

MOTHER: What dear? I'm sorry.

NAIMA: It's you. I said it was you.

MOTHER: (surprised) Me?!

NAIMA: I finally get through to you.

MOTHER: Why are you acting like this? Are you o.k.? Are you taking drugs?

NAIMA: (confused) What?

MOTHER: (to herself a little dazed) Maybe she's pregnant....(to NAIMA) Are you pregnant?

NAIMA: Mom I...

(MOTHER interrupts)

MOTHER: Oh my gosh. Who's the father, when did this happen, how'd this happen? I know, it was that Milo kid wasn't it?

NAIMA: I just came out and said why I was upset. Damn it mother, listen to me.

MOTHER: I'm trying to figure out why you're acting like this.

NAIMA: I just came out and bluntly said it. I'm upset because of you.

MOTHER: I don't understand. Is it because I won't buy you the clothes you want?

NAIMA: (upset) You just don't get it do you?

MOTHER: Is it because of the wine I'm drinking for dinner?

NAIMA: (pleading) It's not just today...

(MOTHER gets up, and interrupts)

MOTHER: Don't start. I'm not in the mood.

NAIMA: (watching her mother carefully) That's the thing. You never are. You never want to talk about it. Well, I think it's time. I'm 18 years old, and I'm an adult. I can carry on a conversation like an adult, with another adult. Now sit down and lets talk. (MOTHER works her way to the cabinet where all of the other bottles of alcohol are located) Mother, come over here and sit down.

MOTHER: (calmly) I need a drink.

NAIMA: No.

MOTHER: Be quiet, Naima.

(Mother opens the cabinet, and pulls out a bottle or two.)

NAIMA: (getting nervous) Mom, I uh.., why don't you, come and um, sit down.

MOTHER: (yelling) I already told you to wait. I just want to get a drink.

NAIMA: Why can't you drink milk or something?

MOTHER: Stop it already. Just leave me alone. Why don't you go to your room or something? Just get away from me.

(Mother opens up the bottle, and takes a drink. She makes a look like something is wrong.)

NAIMA: Mom.....

MOTHER: (suspiciously) ...Naima did....(as Naima talks to her Mother, she checks every bottle, tasting them because none of the bottles are filled with alcohol.)

NAIMA: Mom, I, I'm sorry. I didn't mean to blow this thing out of proportion. I was just having a bad day and I, I guess I needed a reason to you know, and I want to go shopping with y-

(Mother interrupts)

MOTHER: (angrily) Naima, cut the crap. What the hell is your problem? I don't touch your stuff, and you know to stay away from mine. I'm so sick of you. Why don't you just move out? Don't ever ask me for any thing again. You had no right doing this. You're a selfish little brat. All you were thinking about was yourself, and your feelings. I wasn't going to even drink all of that today. Do you know how much money just went down the drain because of you? Damn it.

NAIMA: (screaming) Fine, if that's how you feel...

(Naima is starting to turn around)

MOTHER: (unchanging tone) Where are you going?

NAIMA: Somewhere. I don't know yet. I'm just going. I'm leaving.

MOTHER: Yeah, real smart. Run away from your problems. So where are you going to stay? What about money? You can't survive five minutes with out me.

NAIMA: (sarcastically) Well, it's not like I have a job or anything. Did you know you get paid when you work? And you get money. Surprising isn't it? Plus, grandma told me I could go and live with her and dad if I needed a place to stay.

MOTHER: (getting mad) So go! Do your friends talk to their parents like this? I highly doubt it.

NAIMA: How many friends of mine have you gotten to know? And do you really think my friends mothers have a "little problem" like you do?

MOTHER: (yelling) Just shut the hell up. I don't have to take this from you. I really need a drink.

NAIMA: (confident) Oh yeah. That helps all the time doesn't it, Mother? (Mother glances at her) Go ahead, run from your problems. I'm sure they won't catch up with you in the long run.

MOTHER: SHUT UP, SHUT UP, SHUT UP.

NAIMA: (unchanging expression) Well, it's not like there is any liquor in the bottles.

MOTHER: (annoyed) I didn't notice.

NAIMA: If this is the only way I can stop you from dying, which you are, slowly but surely, then I'll continue to empty out every damn single solitary bottle brought into this hell hole of a house. You can try to hide them, but I know about that secret stash in the closet under all of the blankets. Don't worry about that. I'll turn this house upside down, and inside out if I have to. I'm not going to forget about this that easily, Mother.

MOTHER: (coldly) (As she speaks, she slides down the fridge until she is sitting on the floor, with a bottle in her hands.) This is my house, my stuff. I don't need two mothers. I swear. If you touch one damn thing of mine again, you'll be out of this house so fast your head will spin. And if you hate it here so much, why do you stay? You just clearly pointed out that you can make it on your own. (pause) What's stopping you?

NAIMA: (sadly) I'm not going to abandon you like Daddy did. He couldn't handle you're drinking. But I'm making it a point to help you. This has been going on long enough. If you didn't dwell on the past so much, your drinking wouldn't be so bad.

MOTHER: (depressed) You don't know. You don't know how I felt. My whole world went down the drain. Know one will ever know how I felt, or how I even feel now. All of this pain is to much to handle.

NAIMA: What are you talking about?

(Mother looks like a true drunk now)

MOTHER: You are always saying how you want to be treated like an adult, and can carry on an adult conversation, so let's talk. If you think you are able to handle the truth.

NAIMA: (confused) I don't know what you are talking about. What do you mean, if I can handle the truth?

MOTHER: Your father didn't leave me for another woman. (Naima looks up with big eyes.) Me and your father fell out of love before you were born. Then I found out I was pregnant with you. We decided to stay together for the sake of you. The whole time you were growing up, we never felt an ounce of love for each other. When you turned eighteen is when your father decided to leave. He couldn't just up and leave, so he needed an excuse. That's when he decided to have an affair. It would look more believable.

NAIMA: (anxious) No, no. It's not true. He would never do that to me. You're lying to me. You're just jealous. You think that I love Daddy more than I love you, so you're just making this all up.

MOTHER: (angry) Did you ever notice how he left two days after your birthday? Or how we never did anything together? I know you didn't see any love between the two of us, just like I didn't feel any.

(MOTHER gets up, and puts the bottles down on the counter.)

NAIMA: (hurt) It's not true.

MOTHER: Naima, you're so naive.

NAIMA: How can you say this stuff to me? You're supposed to love me. I don't want to hear anymore of your lies. Think about what you are saying. You're so pathetic. Trying to get me to hate dad 'cauz he left your sorry drunk ass.

(Mother gets up and goes to the table. On her way, she gives Naima a look, sits down and starts drinking the wine. Naima rushes over and tries to grab the bottle, but misses. Naima pulls away, and sits down.)

MOTHER: (frustrated) Damn you, Naima. You just don't know when to quit do you? I'm losing my patience with you. Just get out.

NAIMA: (quick to respond) You don't know what you're saying.

(Mother takes a deep breath, picks up the glass, and takes a drink. There is a lot of tension in the room right now.)

MOTHER: You think I'm a drunk? I can control myself, and what I do. I don't have a problem, you're the ignorant one who thinks I do.

NAIMA: Mother...

(Mother cuts Naima off)

MOTHER: I don't want to hear it anymore.

NAIMA: Do you ever?

MOTHER: I'm a grown woman and I can take care of myself. I don't need you to tell me.

NAIMA: (angry) We'll see how long that lasts. I'll get my things out as soon as possible.

MOTHER: (surprised) Your leaving?

NAIMA: (threatening) If that's what it takes to get away from your drinking and your lies. I always thought that you would stop. That it was for pretend. You always kept the bad things away from me. No one was there to protect you. How could you let this happen? (pauses and looks at the floor, as though ashamed.) To us? When I see you hurting, it kills me inside.   I tried so many things to show you that I love you, and you don't have to go through this alone.

MOTHER: (saddening) By emptying out my bottles?

NAIMA: It prevented you from getting drunk tonight. At least one night is better than none. I tried so hard, so hard. I don't know what else to do. Please stop, Mom. If it's something I said or did, I'm sorry. I'm running low on ideas. So I figure, if I'm gone, you'll miss me like I've missed you for the past 1 1/2 years. Please stop. I love you.... mommy?

(Mother doesn't know what to say, or do. There is a pause as if Naima is waiting for her mom to say something, but Mother has nothing to say. She just continues to look down. Naima keeps looking at her. When she finally realizes Mother isn't going to say anything, she turns and goes into the kitchen.)

MOTHER: (very softly) Naima? I'm...

(Naima cuts her off)

NAIMA: (getting herself a glass of water) I decided to leave.

MOTHER: But I want to tell you...

(NAIMA cuts her off again when she is in the middle of her last word.)

NAIMA: (dazed) I think I've stayed here too long. I'm a grown woman, Mother, and I think it's about time I start to make it on my own. I can probably find a room mate or something.   Me and one of my friends can

even move in together. If not, I can work out something. I don't know.
I just have to get out of here.

MOTHER: (sadly) But, what am I supposed to do?

NAIMA: (coldly) Buy more liquor or something. How am I supposed to
know? It's not my problem. All of a sudden you want my help? How
can you ask for my forgiveness after all you put me through today? If
anything, I should be asking you what I'm supposed to do.

MOTHER: (pleading) We can work this out, honey. It will get better.

NAIMA: Yeah, until tomorrow night. (Mother looks upset. Both of them
are feeling uncomfortable right now. Mother gets up, and puts on her
jacket. She goes to the table and gets her purse. She looks at Naima,
and exits through the door. Naima screams loudly.) Be sure to get
drunk at the bar mom, as usual.

(Naima is upset. She goes into the dining room, and looks at the table.
She sees the bottle of wine, and goes to sit down where her Mother was
just previously sitting. She takes the bottle of wine, and pours 2 glasses
half way. She picks up one, swirls the wine around for a moment, then
smells it. She then toasts with her mother's glass. As she picks it up to
take a drink, her mother walks back in, and sees Naima. Mother looks
down as though ashamed, because she sees Naima with the wine.
Naima continues to sit there. The lights dim, and the curtain falls.)

BARRIERS

by Terrence Sago

Barriers, by Terrence Sago. Zek, a young poet, and his childhood friend Bone, a drug dealer, reminisce about the past. Bone chides Zek for wasting his time on writing poetry. Zek's girlfriend, Tracheal, comes home, and Bone makes it clear he despises their "Waltons" relationship. Zek and Tracheal talk about their hard life together, with jobs and roles in the relationship. Zek reluctantly borrows rent money from Bone. Tracheal comes home from shopping and reveals she was mugged on the street. When Zek takes her to get help, Bone telephones a man and thanks him for hurting Tracheal, then he leaves the apartment. Zek confesses to Tracheal that he has lost his job and borrowed money. Bone confronts the two of them.

ACT 1

(ZEK is sitting on the couch and BONE is sitting on the chair)

BONE: Man, Zek, it's been a long day.

ZEK: Yeah. And it ain't over yet.

BONE: You remember when we were shorties how we got through playing and chasing girls we would go up to Victor Herbert Park and run through the sprinklers.

ZEK: Yeah. And remember how we use to play cops and robbers. how nobody wanted to play the cop. And if you played the cop, you got yo butt kicked.

BONE: Yeah, man, those were the days.

ZEK: You remember how when we played house with the girls. We would play like we were twin brothers

BONE: Marvin and Martin. We'd hop on our bikes and act like they were motorcycles.

ZEK: Playing like we were brothers was easy. It's like we are anyway.

BONE: It's funny how we grow up together and yet we have different views on life.

ZEK: Yeah, that's funny.

BONE: You remember how you couldn't get us apart. Like two peas in a pod.

(SILENCE)

ZEK: What are you saying. We are still two peas. WE would have been like three peas but......

BONE: Come on man, let's not talk about that.

ZEK: I guess you're right. It's just when times get rough. I think about him.

BONE: What do you mean when times get rough. Is something wrong?

ZEK: Sort of. It's a small problem.

BONE: So what's up? What's wrong?

ZEK: I'll tell you later. I got a writing surge coming on.

BONE: Oh, here we go again.

ZEK: Quiet! (ZEK picks his note book and begins to write. BONE gets up and turns on the stereo. The Geto Boys "Straight Gangstarism" is playing in the background. BONE goes to sit back in the chair.)

ZEK: A, check this out. (He begins to read what he had wrote out loud.)
Listen to the sound of the gun.
Listen to the crowd as they duck and run.
Listen to the child as he drops.
Listen to his heart as it stops.
(He stops) Bone, why don't you turn off that mess. I'm trying to concentrate.

BONE: For what? Ain't like you gonna get anywhere. Anyway music relaxes you.

ZEK: Well, it ain't relaxing me. I need peace and quiet to express my view of the ghetto.

BONE: Man, you can cut all that ghetto mess out. Don't nobody want to hear about the ghetto. Not even the people in it.

ZEK: Yeah, like you niggas don't buy gangsta rap.

BONE: That's different. They making money. You ain't making a dime. And what kills me is that you think that writing is gonna be your ticket out of here. (ZEK gets up and turns off the stereo)

ZEK: It is my ticket out. (ZEK goes back and sits back down)

BONE: Now you look. You're stuck just like the rest of us. You ain't getting out no faster than I am.

ZEK:See, that's the problem with every body around here, they think they're stuck. LIke they are afraid to move. Like they're in quicksand.

BONE: You think you got it all figured out, don't you?

ZEK: I do. See writing is my life and when you live for something you are bound to succeed.

BONE: How is poetry your life? You were living way before you knew what poetry was.

ZEK: I thought of all people you would understand.

BONE: All I understand is you ain't making no money. (BONE gets up and turns the stereo back on and goes to sit back down.)

ZEK: Money ain't everything.

BONE: You talk about getting out but you ain't making no money. You go to all those poetry things, work all day and ain't accomplishing nothang. (He reaches in his pocket and pulls out a bank roll of money) See this is where it's at. You need to get down with me so you can make all the ends.

ZEK: Man, I can survive without all that money. I've I've been doing it all my life.

BONE: See you can survive, but with it you can live it up! (BONE puts his money back in his pocket. Zek walks over to the window.)

ZEK: You know as well as I do that type of money only gets you in trouble. Ain't nothing in this ghetto for me. Look around you. This woman out here selling her body, and everybody around here act like they don't see her or even care. Abandon buildings all around, dead or dying trees and grass. People all out on the street corners drunk or getting high. It ain't shit around here to stay for. And yo money ain't helping the community. You selling that poison to your own people. Who in turn are killing and robbing one another for that mess. Man, I'm tired of the same old thing. (ZEK gets up and turns the stereo off and sits back down. Then there is a silence. Tracheal enters the room)

TRACHEAL: I'm home.

ZEK: How was school.

TRACHEAL: Fine. Let me tell you what happen. I was.......

BONE: Ya'll need to cut all that phony stuff out.

ZEK: What are you talking about?

BONE: Trying to act like ya'll all that. Like ya'll the Waltons or something. I"m home, Pa. How was your day, Ma? Does it matter, I'm home now with my loving family.

TRACHEAL: (In a harsh voice) What are you doing here.

BONE: I ain't here for you.

TRACHEAL: That's good. Zek, you need to leave him alone. I don't understand why you hang out with him.

ZEK: He's my boy. Anyways, I don't pick your friends for you.

BONE: Look Zek you don't have to say nothing. I'm up. I don't have to listen to your so called woman. (He turns to exit and stops) And under stand this, I was his friend long before you were his woman. (He exits)

TRACHEAL: Why do you hang with him? You know he ain't nothing but a petty crack pusher. He's gonna get you in trouble, or even hurt.

ZEK: Why are you tripping. Don't you think I know what he's all about. I just can't let go of a friendship just cause you tell me to. I'm trying to change him. I know there is some good under all that phony stuff he shows ya'll.

TRACHEAL: You've been trying to change him since I've known ya'll. He ain't gonna change. You know how they say you can't change someone that don't want to change. And you talking about you chang- ing him, but eventually he's going to change you.

ZEK: I'm too strong for that. I've worked too hard to get here to let him pull me down. (He sighs) Alright, if Bone doesn't straighten up I'm gonna kick him to the curb.

TRACHEAL: It's about time you begin to see the light. He wasn't doing nothing but holding you back. (She walks over to the couch and grabs his hand and pulls him up) Look baby I'm not trying to be harsh but I want you to make it, and he ain't helping you. (She gives him a hug and they both smile and sit on the couch) How's your writing coming along.

ZEK: All right I guess. Why don't you read this and tell me what you think. (He hands her his notebook. She reads the poem out loud)

TRACHEAL: Listen to the sound of the gun.
Listen as the crowd ducks and run.
Listen to the child as he drops.
Listen to his heart as it stops.
Listen as another dream comes to an end.
Listen to the cries of his friends.
Listen as the community points the blame.
Listen as the politicians treat it as a game.
Listen, all this senseless violence must end.
Because the next victim might be one of your friends.

(She stops and smiles) Zek, this is nice. But, uh, when are you gonna write something about me?

ZEK: I didn't know that I needed to write about you to show you how much I care. You know you mean the world to me.

TRACHEAL: Yeah right. So how was work today?

ZEK: You know the same old same old. I'm thinking about quitting.

TRACHEAL: Why?

ZEK: Well, I'm not really having fun.

TRACHEAL: A job is not supposed to be fun. What are you going to do for money if you quit. You know we are having a hard time now, so why quit?

ZEK: I don't know. But I shouldn't have trouble finding another job.

TRACHEAL: Zek, just stay there until you get something better.

ZEK: I will try. Anyway, finish what you were saying earlier.

TRACHEAL: When?

ZEK: You know. What you were talking about earlier.

TRACHEAL: Aw yeah. I was saying that I had seen my best friend Reyna. She was telling me that her job was hiring and she said that they start people off at $19.36 an hour.

ZEK: Where do she work?

TRACHEAL: Let me finish. I ask her if she could get you a job down there. She said that she knew a couple of people and she would see what she could do.

ZEK: Where?

TRACHEAL: She works for the city. At the main library on State street.

ZEK: Doing what?

TRACHEAL: She works on the central loading docks.

ZEK: So when is next time you'll talk to her?

TRACHEAL: I don't know. But she said she will call you tonight to let you know what's up.

ZEK: Cool. That'll be right on time.

TRACHEAL: Right on time for what?

ZEK: Oh, nothing. So what are you cooking for dinner.

TRACHEAL: Nigga please. You've been here all this time and you ain't started to cook dinner.

ZEK: Nah. I was waiting on you.

TRACHEAL: Waiting on me. You must be smoking. How long have you been here?

ZEK: For awhile now.

TRACHEAL: What? You got off work early.

ZEK: Yeah. Sort of.

TRACHEAL: You've been here all this time and you ain't cook. You must not be hungry. Oh, you expecting me to cook.

ZEK: All right, I get the picture. So what do you want for dinner?

TRACHEAL: Can you make filet mignon. (She starts laughing)

ZEK: Nah, but can you settle for cube steak and rice?

TRACHEAL: I guess that'll do.

ZEK: It betta.

TRACHEAL: So, Zek. Why did you leave work early today?

ZEK: No reason. I, I just wasn't feeling good.

TRACHEAL: Are you alright? You've been leaving work a lot lately.

ZEK: Yeah, I'm straight. I haven't been feeling well.

TRACHEAL: Maybe you need to go to the doctor.

ZEK: I'll be alright, I just need to get some rest. You keeping me up at night just ain't cool.

TRACHEAL: You know you like every minute of it.

ZEK: I ain't complaining. (He gives her a kiss on the cheek) Let me go get supper ready for my baby.

(He gets up, begins to exit)

TRACHEAL: Zek. (He stops) I love you.

ZEK: I love you too.

(She smiles)

TRACHEAL: Nigga, why you lying? You don't love me, you just love my doggie-style.

ZEK: You're a trip.

(There is a knock at the door)

ZEK: Who is it?

BONE: (Off stage) Bone.

ZEK: Come in.

(BONE enters)

TRACHEAL: What are you doing here? Don't you got a home?

BONE: I ain't here to see you.

TRACHEAL: Zek, if you don't tell him, I will.

ZEK: Calm your nerves.

TRACHEAL: Only way I'll calm my nerves is to leave ya'll two buddies alone. (She storms out. ZEK gets up)

BONE: Peace! Man you beta check yo so called girl.

ZEK: Look man. She'll be alright.

BONE: I know she will. (Pause) So what did you want to talk to me about. (He sits in the chair)

ZEK: That's alright now.

BONE: I've known you long enough to know that everything ain't all right. Look at that face. I'm yo boy. I know you got a problem. I'm gonna do my best to help you solve it. (He sits on the couch)

ZEK: I'm cool.

BONE: Yeah right. If you can't tell me, who can you tell?

ZEK: O.k. Well nah. (Pause) Look Bone, we're short on the rent.

BONE: Do Ms. goody-two-shoes know?

ZEK: Nah! I can't tell her.

BONE: How much are you short.

ZEK: Four C-notes.

BONE: Now see, if you were down with me you wouldn't have this problem. But nah. You trying to be good. Don't you understand. That writing shit ain't moving. (He reaches in his pocket and pulls out his money) Well since you're my boy, I guess I could loan it to you.

ZEK: Nah, that's all right. We'll make it.

BONE: Yeah right. Stop being stubborn. Fifty, one hundred, one fifty, two hundred, three hundred, three fifty, four hundred. (He puts his money back in his pocket, and hands ZEK the money he counted out but, ZEK refuses)

BONE: Here take it.

ZEK: I really shouldn't take it.

BONE: Man take it. It ain't like it's coming from a stranger.

ZEK: I guess you're right. (BONE gives him the money)

ZEK: I'm gonna pay you back as soon as I can.

BONE: Don't worry about it.

(TRACHEAL comes in with a look of pain and horror on her face)

ZEK: What's wrong?

TRACHEAL: I, I, I....

ZEK: Calm down. Now what happened?

TRACHEAL: Some man just robbed me.

BONE: Do you know who it was?

TRACHEAL: I've seen him around before.

ZEK: What did he look like?

TRACHEAL: He was tall, and he had on a gray sweater with some type of letter on it. He was real dark.

ZEK: Did he have a gun?

TRACHEAL: Nah, but he put a knife to my throat.

ZEK: He didn't hurt you, did he?

TRACHEAL: Nah, I'm alright. (She begins crying)

ZEK: He's probably a hype. (He gets up and hugs TRACHEAL) Baby, calm down. It will be alright.

BONE: So what are you gonna do about it?

ZEK: What do you want me to do?

BONE: You need to go out and get the nigga who did that to her.

ZEK: You know I'm not gonna find him. He's probably gone by now.

BONE: Nah, you just hoping he's gone. Man, I can't believe you.

ZEK: Believe what?

BONE: Yo woman just got robbed and you sittin here like nothin happened.

ZEK: What do you want me to do? She didn't get hurt. Ain't no use for me to go runnin out there lookin for trouble.

BONE: Man, you are a trip.

ZEK: I ain't no trip. I just got better things to do. (He gets up and holds TRACHEAL in his arms) Why don't I take you in the back so you can get some rest? (TRACHEAL and ZEK exit. BONE sits on the couch, picks up the phone and dials a number)

BONE: Yeah, can I speak to Lil Mike? Yeah, Mike, what's up? (Pause) It's me, Bone. Is Corey in the room with you? (Pause) Ask him did he take care of that for me. (Pause) Put him on the phone. (Pause) Yeah, Corey. Are you sure you got Tracheal? (Pause) Yeah, he's my boy, but I can't stand her Puerto Rican butt. Don't worry about all that. Lil Mike gonna pay you. Put him back on the phone. (Pause) Yeah. Check this out. I just had Corey stick up Tracheal. I want you to pay him. (Pause) Pop him. (Pause) Yeah. Hold on.

(ZEK walks in. BONE holds the phone down)

BONE: Zek, you're back quick. How's Tracheal?

ZEK: Like you really care.

BONE: Well, I really don't, I just want to know.

ZEK: She's alright I guess. (Sits on couch)

BONE: Let me get off the phone. (Picks up the phone) Yeah, Mike. I'm about to go, but page me when you take care of that. (Hangs up the phone) Why didn't you go look for that guy?

ZEK: I don't want to talk about it.

BONE: You never want to talk. You always grab yo pen and paper and begin to write. That writing stuff ain't gettin you nowhere.

ZEK: I said I don't want to talk about it.

BONE: What is yo problem? Your girl gets robbed and you just sittin here like nothin's wrong.

ZEK: What do you want me to do?

BONE: I don't know.

ZEK: (ZEK picks up the phone) I got it.

BONE: What are you doing?

ZEK: Callin' the cops.

BONE: Are you crazy? (He gets up and grabs the phone) Tracheal! (Pause) Tracheal!

TRACHEAL:(Offstage) Yeah!

ZEK: What are you callin her for? (TRACHEAL enters)

TRACHEAL: What's wrong?

BONE: He's in here tryin to call the police. They ain't gonna help you. You don't need them. They can't do nothin for you.

ZEK: It ain't gonna hurt to try.

BONE: Then what?

ZEK: I don't know.

BONE: We'll take care of it. Just you and me. Like we used to do.

TRACHEAL: Zek ain't goin' nowhere. He might get killed or something.

BONE: Man, we all gonna die. Some sooner than others, but we all will die. I've realized death is inevitable and so are dreams.

TRACHEAL: What are you talking about dreams? You don't have any. You run around like you already own the world.

ZEK: Now ain't the time for nonsense.

BONE: Nah, Zek, let me respond. I don't own the world now, but that is my dream. To be larger than life. To rise to the occasion. I've grown. (He reaches in his pocket and pulls his money out) And this is what's gonna help me. I'm gonna take this world by storm and grasp it in my hand like a tiny ball.

TRACHEAL: See, that's your problem. You're too...(Interrupted by the sound of a pager)

BONE: Look, I'd love to stay and chat, but I've gotta go. (He looks at his pager) Zek, you comin'?

ZEK: Nah, I'm gonna stay here.

BONE: Alright. I'll be back.

ZEK: Cool. (BONE exits)

TRACHEAL: Boy, he is nerve wracking.

ZEK: You gotta understand...

TRACHEAL: Understand what? He thinks he's the bomb. All he is is a two bit drug pusher who gets his kicks off other people's pain.

ZEK: It ain't like that.

TRACHEAL: Why are you always taking up for him? He's grown. He knows right from wrong and he knows he's responsible for his own actions.

ZEK: Baby, you just a little uptight. Why don't you go run some warm water in the tub so you can relax. And when you're finished I'll give you a massage.

TRACHEAL: Don't be trying to treat me like a little girl.

ZEK: I'm sorry. It's just that so much has happened today.

TRACHEAL: Maybe you're right. It's been a long day. (TRACHEAL exits. ZEK grabs his notebook and throws it across the room.)

ZEK:(To himself out loud) Man. Life doesn't make sense. It always looks like I have everything in my reach and it slips away. I got to get out of this hell hole everybody calls a ghetto. It's sucking me in. It has a hold of the inner me and it's tearing him apart. I'm supposed to be the man of the house but I can't ever control what goes on around me. I can't ever protect my girl on the street. And my boy, well, my supposed to be boy is trying to get me in some mess. He knows I ain't about that. All these negative things surrounding me. There isn't one good thing. Oh, yes there is. I'm alive. But that isn't so hot. My life is like an accident waitin' to happen. Maybe Bone is right. We all die. I just wish I could die sooner to escape this hell hole. Tracheal, come in here for a second. (TRACHEAL enters)

TRACHEAL: What's up?

ZEK: You know I love you.

TRACHEAL: I love you too.

ZEK: I'm tryin to get us outta here. I don't want our future family surrounded by all this confusion.

TRACHEAL: With me working and going to school and you working, going to school and writing, something good is gonna come out of that.

ZEK: Well, that's what I want to talk about. I'm not working anymore.

TRACHEAL: What?

ZEK: I lost my job about two weeks ago. I've been trying to find another.

TRACHEAL: Why didn't you tell me?

ZEK: I was gonna tell you as soon as I found another one.

TRACHEAL: How are we gonna pay the bills?

ZEK: I borrowed some money from Bone.

TRACHEAL: You what? Zek, I'm disappointed in you. How could you do this to me? How could you keep something like this from me? (Silence) You're gonna have to give that money back.

ZEK: How are we gonna pay the rent?

TRACHEAL: I don't know, we just gonna have to make it.

ZEK: I had a hard enough time trying to accept the money, now you want me to give it back.

TRACHEAL: Zek, sometimes it takes something like this to make you strive hard. Look, we've paid our rent every month. I think this landlord would understand if we tell her that we're short.

ZEK: I guess you're right.

TRACHEAL: You gotta come up off that pride thing. This is the Nineties. Ain't nothin wrong with you takin care of me, but when things get a little rough that's where I step in to give you a hand.

ZEK: I guess you are right.

TRACHEAL: I know I'm right. (They both smile) Now you better start telling me when you need that hand. (There is a knock at the door)

ZEK: Who is it?

BONE: It's me! Bone.

ZEK: Come in. (BONE enters)

BONE: You alright, man?

ZEK: Yeah, I'm straight.

BONE: Well anyway, I found out who did it...(Interrupted)

TRACHEAL: Who?

BONE: You always try and put me out, but now you need me. Ain't that a trip.

ZEK: Enough of all that. Who did it?

BONE: Well, since you my boy I'll tell you. (Pause) It was Corey.

ZEK:(Surprised) Corey! Ain't he one of your boys?

BONE: Yeah.

TRACHEAL: I knew I had seen him before.

ZEK: Are you sure it was him?

BONE: Ain't that what I said? He told Mike, and Mike told me.

ZEK: Wait til I get my hands on him...

BONE: You don't have to worry about that.

ZEK: Why not?

BONE: Cause he's in the hospital.

TRACHEAL: He is? How?

BONE: He got shot in the chest.

ZEK: By who?

BONE: I had Mike do it.

ZEK: For what?

BONE: For messin' with yo girl.

ZEK:What type of stuff is that? You didn't have to do that.

BONE: What? A minute ago you were talking about killing him and now that he's damn near dead, there you're tripping.

ZEK: I was just talking.

BONE: Well that's what I thought you wanted.

TRACHEAL: I told you he was nothing but trouble. (She sits on couch and puts her head down in disbelief)

BONE: How you gonna trip? I did that for you.

ZEK: You what? I could have taken care of it myself. I didn't need you to do that.

BONE: Yeah, right.

ZEK: What do you mean by that?

BONE: Don't play. I've done things like that for you all my life.

ZEK: I'm grown now. It's time out for those "I've got yo back" games.

BONE: I guess you're right, but you know as well as I do that you ain't never played those type of games. You have always run from your problems. Oops, I mean, you escape, as you call it.

ZEK: I never had time to play stupid stuff like that. Life is too short to be trying to knock every problem down head on.

BONE: Nigga, you ain't never knocked a problem down head on. How did you wind up living here? Why don't you talk to your family? (Raises her head up)

TRACHEAL: What family? He never said nothing about his family.

ZEK: All that's not important.

BONE: Oh, you didn't tell her.

TRACHEAL: Tell me what?

BONE: Ask him why he left one side of the city and came over here.

TRACHEAL: Why?

ZEK: I got into a little trouble.

TRACHEAL: A little trouble. What kind of trouble?

BONE: Since he's so reluctant to tell you, I will.

ZEK: It ain't her business.

BONE: If you plan on being with her for the rest of your life, what are you scared of?

ZEK: Nothing.

BONE: Well, let me tell her then.

ZEK: Go ahead, I don't care.

BONE: Ms. Tracheal, his cousin got killed about two years ago. He found out who did it, so he got a gun. Once he got the gun I guess he thought he was bad. He went out to find the guys who did it. Well, he saw them on the corner of Madison and Oakley. Without thinking he just started shooting. Before you know it he had let out a sixteen shot nine and didn't hit nobody. Well the guys found out it was him and they began looking for him to kill. He ran. Just like a chicken. He left everything behind. His family, his friends and his life. He left it all.

TRACHEAL: Why didn't you tell me that?

ZEK: It wasn't important.

BONE: Oh, it gets better. Guess who had to bail him out? Me, good old Bone.

ZEK: I didn't need you.

BONE: Yeah, right. If it wasn't for me you might be dead. Oh yeah, did he tell you about the time he tried selling drugs? That was the stupidest thing I had ever seen. Your past is just as dark as mine. And you try to act like you're so much better than I am. Man, you need to face reality.

ZEK: That was the past. I had enough sense to change. You need to face reality. Everything's changing. The people, the neighborhoods, the government. And they ain't gonna take that stuff off of you. They gonna come down on you like a ton of bricks. See, you're not stuck in the ghetto, you're stuck in the past. Things don't happen the same way anymore. Niggas don't fight, they shoot. Nobody smokes joints anymore, it's blunts. And I can't figure out what my past has to do with you shooting someone.

BONE: I did it for you.

ZEK: If you were a friend you wouldn't have done it.

BONE: Oh well, it's over.

ZEK: Nah, it ain't over. You ain't getting me caught up in nothing.

BONE: Aw, you mister big stuff now.

ZEK: Nah, but I don't need no trouble and you're nothing but trouble.

BONE: So what are you saying?

ZEK: If you're going to be trouble, I don't need you.

BONE: Zek, you know trouble is my joy.

ZEK: Your joy is something I don't need. (Pause) Bone, why don't you leave.

BONE: So you putting me out.

ZEK: Yeah, and don't come back because I've realized I don't need you.

BONE: So you're finally listening to her. What, she controls you now?

ZEK: Maybe.

BONE: Ain't this about a...

ZEK: Nah. It ain't. I just rather for someone good guiding me than someone bad holding me back.

BONE: So it's like that.

ZEK: Yeah it is.

BONE: So what if I don't leave?

ZEK: Then I would have to call the law and tell them your little secret.

BONE: You wouldn't dare. (ZEK walks over and gets the phone)

ZEK: Try me.

BONE: All right. Cool. But since we were shedding secrets, I've got another one. I'm the one who had yo girl stuck up. (TRACHEAL jumps up from the couch in an uproar)

TRACHEAL: I told you he was nothing but trouble. You should've left him alone a long time ago.

BONE: Broad, you better sit yo butt down before you get hurt. See, there's one thing you should know. I never liked yo Puerto Rican butt. Zek could have done betta if he had a black woman.

TRACHEAL: You so phony. You don't like me because of my race? I ought to cut your throat. But you know I ain't gonna stoop to your level.

BONE: Anyway! You just like Zek now, too scared to face what you feel. Y'all make a great couple. Two big chickens. (TRACHEAL slaps BONE)

ZEK: Tracheal! (TRACHEAL sits down again)

BONE: Yeah! That's it! Like Toni Braxton said, "Let it Flow". Now you got more courage than your man.

ZEK: Now you know you betta leave.

BONE: It has come down to this. You've picked her over me. We've been friends long before she came into the picture. Remember how it used to be? Just you and me. Zek, you know you are all I got.

ZEK: You should have thought of that. Why would you play me like that? Betta yet, why would you play yourself?

BONE: I didn't mean it. You know I've been this way all my life.

ZEK: It's time for you to change.

BONE: You are the only family I got.

ZEK: Use your money to buy a family.

BONE: I didn't mean for it to come down to this. I just wanted her out of the picture. I didn't know she meant a lot to you.

ZEK: See, that's your problem, you don't think. The world doesn't revolve around you and your money. It takes more than money. It takes someone that cares, and you, my friend, don't care about anyone. Nobody but your damn self.

BONE: You know I care about you.

ZEK: Nah, you don't care. Because if you did, you wouldn't have done Tracheal like that. You wouldn't have tried to pull me into some mess.

BONE: Zek, just forgive me for it. You know, like when we were little kids. I would do something and you'd forgive me for it.

ZEK: Them days are over. We ain't kids anymore.

BONE: It won't happen again.

ZEK: I know. Because you gotta go.

BONE: You're for real, aren't you? (Pause) All right, I'm up. (He turns and walks toward the exit and stops) If you need me, I'll be around. (BONE exits)

TRACHEAL: I told you he was nothing but trouble. It's about time you open your eyes. (She gets up and hugs him and kisses him on the cheek) Oh, I forgot my bath water. (TRACHEAL exits. ZEK walks over to the couch and gazes across the audience. Then he sits down. Looks through the papers on the table and picks one up. He begins to read a poem out loud.)

ZEK: "STUCK"

"Why do you think we're stuck in a place that has no gates.
In a place that has no barriers, which society calls the ghetto.
Why do you think we can only go so far up the financial ladder.
Trapped in a financial pothole in which society calls poverty.
Why do you try and hold someone back and keep them from succeed-
ing and reaching their goals in life.
Tripping each other up, when we are all running the same race to get
ahead.
Why are we falling victim to the hands of our own people.
It seems if no one cares.
Why do you think we are stuck.
Well if you think we are stuck then you are.
You're stuck only if you stay........
(He pause and gazes out over the audience)
I'm not staying.

(Blackout)

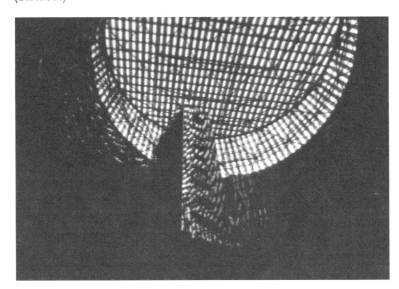

An excerpt from

Bird Watching

By Brian Patrick Norton

Bird Watching, by Brian Patrick Norton. CT and his best friend, Carly sit on a beach and watch the world pass by. Carly works hard to be "one of the boys," laughing at CT's gross-outs and sexist comments about scantily-clad women who pass by ("the North American big-breasted cheerleader chick"), as well as his hilariously sarcastic outlook on life in general. Carly patiently listens as CT describes his nonexistent love life and his disdain for her smoking. We learn that they go to parties together as friends, not as a romantic couple. It becomes clear that Carly is playing along with CT's commentary for a reason.

(Lights reveal CT and CARLY sitting in the two lawn chairs under the beach umbrella. CT is looking over the audience through his binoculars while CARLY reads a thick paperback novel)

CARLY: (Placing novel in her lap) I hate this beach. (CT ignores and continues looking)

CARLY: (louder) I said, I hate this beach. (CT ignores and continues looking)

CARLY: (Waving her hand in front of the binoculars) CT! Earth to CT! Come in CT!

CT: So?

CARLY: So, why are we here?

CT: (Sarcastically) Gee, I don't know. It's either because of the seagulls or the hundreds of beautiful blondes that prance across this beach everyday. I wonder...

CARLY: Oh, I see. I'm sitting here bored stiff so you can sit here stiff as a board.

CT: (Still looking through his binoculars smiling) Ain't life grand?

CARLY: I've got to get you a woman.

CT: Good luck

(Short pause for subject change)

CARLY: So, wood-meister, what am I supposed to do while you're entertaining Mr. Happy?

CT: I dunno. Go swimming.

CARLY: Hell yeah! Wonderful idea, Einstein! Ninety percent of the water is raw sewage. I might as well go home and do swan dives into my toilet!

CT: (Still looking through the binoculars) Hey, whatever floats your boat.

CARLY: You are a sick little man.

CT: Love you too.

CARLY: So, what the hell are you looking at?

CT: (sarcastically) Birds.

CARLY: (playing along) Oh really? So, tell me Mr. Birdwatcher, what

lovely specimens are we observing today?

CT: The North American Big Breasted Cheerleader Chick. It is commonly found at the beach or in the back seat of some muscle bound football players car.

CARLY: Let me see. (CT hands CARLY the binoculars and points out over the audience)

CT: That one. Right there.

CARLY: Her?

CT: Yeah, her.

CARLY: She's got flabby thighs.

CT: What?!

CARLY: She's got flabby thighs.

CT: No she doesn't!

CARLY: She's got a fat, dumpy butt, too. (CT takes the binoculars back and looks for himself)

CT: She does not have a...Wow! What a dumpy butt!

CARLY: Told ya!

CT: I should really start looking in the southern hemisphere more often.

CARLY: What would you do without me?

CT: Date doglike, dumpy butt chicks.

CARLY: You do that anyway.

CT: See, I don't need you. You're useless

CARLY: (sweetly) But you love me don't you?

CT: (sarcastically) Not the way I love my other chicks.

CARLY: You mean the non-existent, doglike, dumpy butt chicks.

CT: Hey! My dumpy butt chicks are real!

CARLY: Maybe in those pretty little dreams you've been having.

CT: (laughing) You mean the ones where I'm on a pirate ship and all these chicks are tearing off their...

CARLY: (interrupting) Thank you! That's very nice... Thank you very much.

CT: Besides not all my girls are doglike. What about Helen?

CARLY: Helen Jacobson?

CT: Yeah, what's wrong with her?

CARLY: She was a fox except for that little mountain she called a nose.

CT: There was nothing wrong with her nose!

CARLY: No, not unless she smacked you with it.

CT: It wasn't that long.

CARLY: Are you kidding? She nearly poked you eyes out every time you kissed her.

CT: Okay, she had a big nose. That doesn't make her doglike.

CARLY: No, but the way she ate did.

CT: What was wrong with the way she ate?

CARLY: Nothing. If she were a canine, but unfortunately, as a human, it is expected that most of the food gets inside your mouth. Remember, last year at your birthday party? She could hardly eat a single piece of pizza without getting it all over herself. She was totally revolting.

CT: Still, that just makes her-

CARLY: (interrupting) Doglike.

CT: Yeah, I guess so. Speaking of doglike chicks, where the hell were you last night? I called you, like, thirty times and you weren't home.

CARLY: (Slightly embarrassed) I was, um busy.

CT: Doing what?

CARLY: Um, I dunno. Just busy.

CT: (smiling) On the rag again, huh?

CARLY: Yeah, being a woman sucks.

CT: (mimicking CARLY) Being a woman sucks.

CARLY: Shut up! You don't understand. It really sucked this time, because my dad was in the bathroom. and you know how long it takes him in there. It's like once he gets in there, he doesn't want to come out. So, I was stuck in my room the whole time.

CT: Why didn't you just knock on the door and ask him to come out?

CARLY: (sarcastically) Oh yeah, why didn't I think of that. "Daddy, chunks of blood and flesh are flying out of my body, would you hurry in the bathroom please?"

CT: (A disgusted look on his face) You didn't have to get so graphic.

CARLY: You asked for it. (changing the subject) Anyway, why were you calling me?

CT: Oh, nuthin really. Just wanted you to come to some party with me. It sucked, you would of hated it.

CARLY: Why?

CT: It was just some preppie party. You wouldn't have liked it. Just a bunch of preppies doing their typical preppie crap.

CARLY: Get any numbers?

CT: Four or five, but I ain't gonna call any of them.

CARLY: Why not?

CT: Because, we're talking about preppie girls. These chicks only give you their numbers as a formality. They don't really want you to call them. They just want you right here, right now. They'll love you and then they'll leave you. I've just got too much self respect for that. I want a long, meaningful relationship, not just one night of passion.

CARLY: (smiling) Dirty underwear, huh?

CT: (embarrassed) Um, no.

CARLY: C'mon fess up! Were they just a day old or were they all disgusting and-

CT: (interrupting, still embarrassed) The washing machine is broken. It wasn't my fault. I...

CARLY: (laughing giddily) I knew it! Oh, my God! I can't believe it!

CT: (angrily) Hey, listen you idiot, it's a matter of principle. I was-

CARLY: (interrupting) A matter of principle! (Becomes hysterical with laughter) How stupid can you be?! I mean, you're there, she's there! What's wrong...(Begins laughing harder)

(C.T.'s facial expressions show him becoming madder and madder. CARLY notices and decides to calm down)

CARLY: I'm sorry. I just can't believe you gave up getting some because of an unwashed pair of Jockeys.

CT: Hanes.

CARLY: Hanes. Sorry.

CT: (coolly) Apology accepted. (C.T. reaches into the cooler and pulls out the hotdog. He unwraps it and begins to eat.)

CARLY: That's disgusting.

CT: What?

CARLY: That revolting piece of crap that you happen to be shoving down your throat.

CT: My hotdog?

CARLY: If that's what they're calling crap these days. Do you even know what's in that stuff?

CT: Yeah.

CARLY: What?

CT: Food.

CARLY: I'll tell you what's in that. They take whatever is leftover from the pig. You know, the stuff that isn't taken out for porkchops and stuff like that. Then, they grind it up into a disgusting mush. Then, they pack the mush into a piece of pigskin, which is nothing more than a piece of shoe leather if you really take the time to think about it. So, all you're eating is shoe leather and pig guts. Yum, nothing like hog intestine and Reeboks in the morning.

CT: (smiling) Nope, this is a beef hotdog.

CARLY: (disgusted) Retard.

(C.T. picks up his binoculars and resumes his girl watching.)

CARLY: (loudly, mocking) Boing! Bring on the lumberjacks, there's wood to be cut!

CT: I'm simply taking in the beauty of my environment. (short pause) You pervert!

CARLY: (giggling) So, Senor Birdwatcher, what fine species are we observing now?

CT: The beautiful North American Prom Queen. It can easily be identified by it's perfectly toned muscles, beautiful measurements and gleaming white teeth.

CARLY: Oh fascinating, let me see.

(C.T. hands CARLY the binoculars)

CARLY: Ouch!! Nice, very nice. That's nearly flawless! Sick her C.T.! Sick her!

CT: Naw, I don't want to get up.

CARLY: (surprised) What?! You wuss! What's the matter with you? What are you afraid of? Are you ... oh yeah! Dirty underwear! (starts laughing)

CT: (smiling, smugly) I'm not wearing any. (CARLY goes silent, short pause)

CARLY: Pervert. (C.T. breaks out laughing)

CT: Lettin' it all hang out!

CARLY: (disgusted) Now I have that image stuck in my head.

CT: (laughing) Bet you're happy.

CARLY: (starts laughing) Pervert! Pervert! Pervert!! (CARLY begins to slap C.T. jokingly. A playful slap fight breaks out. Slap fight ends. The two are laughing. CARLY lights a cigarette. C.T. yanks it from her mouth and hurls it across the stage.)

CARLY: (angrily) What the hell is wrong with you?

CT: When the hell did you start smoking?

CARLY: Yesterday, why?

CT: Why!? Since then you have most likely smoked a pack and a half. That has probably taken about three hours off your life. So what if you're supposed to die two hours from now? Guess what? You're dead already! (Begins yelling) Besides that, do you know what's in that crap?! Tar!! You're taking the same crud they make streets out of and putting it in your mouth. You won't even sit on the sidewalk and now you're sucking on part of the street! And while I'm on a roll, let's talk about carbon monoxide. The stuff you're breathing in is the same crap that comes out of a car! (Still yelling. Now brutally sarcastic) Yummy! That sounds delicious! I've got a great idea! Let's go back to my place and suck on the tail pipe of my dad's Chevy van while we eat little chunks of the street. Hell! While we're at it why don't we drink anti-freeze out of a Jack Daniels bottle and squirt WD-40 up our noses! Wow, sounds like a party to me! (C.T. stops to catch his breath. CARLY replies calmly.)

CARLY: But those are Virginia Slims.

CT: (very sarcastically) Oh, I'm sorry! I thought all you were doing was turning your legs into huge sacks of mush! I didn't realize you were smoking the cigarettes that give you a trimmer waist line, bigger breasts and make you irresistible to the opposite sex! Go ahead and get down, you sexy mama!

CARLY: (striking a pose) Don't hate me because I'm beautiful.

CT: (a mock cherub voice) I know you love me. (Carly kisses C.T. on the cheek)

CT: Ewww! Nicotine breath! You're disgusting! (CARLY makes a large smile and giggles. C.T. points at her teeth)

CT: You've got teeth stains already. See, you're an addict!

CARLY: (smiling) Yeah, but I'm the sexiest addict you've ever seen.

CT: (sarcastically) Yes, you are one sexy mama.

CARLY: See, you do love me.

CT: I don't love you, I just love your doggie-style.

CARLY: Pig.

CT: How the hell did we get on this subject? I thought we were talking about your nasty habit.

CARLY: We were. But now we're talking about how sexy I am.

CT: What about me? I'm all that and a bag of chips.

CARLY: (giggling)Yeah, I guess you're pretty hot for a craterfacer with flabby pecks .

CT: (Pretending that his feeling are hurt) Why are you so mean to me?

CARLY: (sarcastically)Because I love you.

CT: (irritated) Will you quit saying that.

CARLY: What?

CT: People always say that, no one ever means it.

CARLY: Geez, I was just goofing around. What's your probl-

CT: (interrupting) I'll tell you what my problem is. I'm tired of always hearing people say stuff they don't mean. I love you! I love you! All the time! People always say it whether they are friends with you or are infatuated with you or even if they are only asphyxiated with you, they still-

CARLY: What did you just say?!

CT: I just said that-

CARLY: (interrupting) Did you say "asphyxiated"?

CT: Yeah, so?

CARLY: So, I sincerely doubt that any asphyxiated people are going to say "I love you"

CT: (smugly) Oh really, why?

CARLY: Well, it's just a hunch, but it could be because they can't breathe. (A confused look crosses C.T.'s face)

CARLY: (laughing) Don't try to sound smart. You'll hurt yourself.

CT: (still confused) I don't get... What are you... Oh, forget it. You're an idiot!

CARLY: (sweetly) Love you, too.

CT: (coolly) Shut up. (CARLY giggles softly)

CARLY: While we're talking about the birds and the bees, I-

CT: (interrupting, irritated) I don't wanna talk about this anymore!

CARLY: (giggling) You're funny when you're angry. You get all tense and your face gets all- (In order to change the subject, C.T. interrupts with the monologue from "Taxi Driver")

CT: (in a phony Italian accent) You talkin' to me? Are you talkin' to me? Well, I'm the only -

CARLY: (interrupting) No!! I hate that!

CT: What's your problem?

CARLY: My problem is that every guy I've ever come into contact with has done that stupid bit for me over and over and over again! And I'm just supposed to sit there and laugh and pretend it is the first time I've heard it, well no thank you! I hate it! I hate it! I hate Robert Deniro for saying it! I hate that stupid movie! I hate taking cabs because of that movie! Don't ever say that to me again! Have I made myself perfectly clear!? (short pause)

CT: Um, sorry.

CARLY: (calming down) It's okay, it's not your fault. You're a male. The extra baggage in your crotch prevents you from thinking and functioning like a normal human being.

CT: (confused) Um, thanks. I think.

CARLY: Anytime, bucko!

CT: Don't call me "bucko"!

CARLY: (poking fun) What's wrong C.T.? Don't you like the name "Bucko"!?

CT: It sounds like the name of a porno star.

CARLY: Well, you're the expert. (short pause) Pervert!

CT: Just telling it like it is.

CARLY: I'm sure you are. Anyway, I've got something to ask you.

CT: The answer is yes.

CARLY: What?!

CT: I said yes. I do believe that aliens created humans to colonize this planet.

CARLY: That's not what I wanted to ask.

CT: But that's the answer you're going to get, take it or leave it.

CARLY: Leave it.

CT: Okay, but remember it was a choice.

CARLY: (annoyed) Can you get serious, please?

CT: Not unless we're talking about either aliens or chicks. Otherwise, I'm not interested.

CARLY: It's about chicks.

CT: (loudly)Boda-bing, boda-boom! Okay, I'm interested.

CARLY: Okay, are you calm?

CT: Sure.

CARLY: Alright, here's the scenario. Let's say one of those chicks you were drooling over came over here and asked you out. Okay, you go out, you party and then at the end of the night she tells you that she loves you. What are you gonna do? Honestly.

CT: (thinks for a moment) Hmmm. I could probably drown her and put her out of the misery that comes from leading a mindless, pathetic life.

CARLY: Will you please get serious!

CT: I am serious! The girl is obviously a complete and total moron. One, for being so forward as to tell me that on the first date. And two, for being blind enough to buy into love in the first place. The only reason any girl would ever tell a guy that is to get him in the sack.

CARLY: (needling him) And that isn't good enough for you?

CT: No, that isn't good enough for me! I mean sure I wanna get laid just a much as the next guy, but I've still got standards. Hell, if I'm gonna get it on with some slut, then I at least want her to have enough self respect to admit she's a slut. I don't want her to go and tell a lie to me? It's not going to change my mind about anything.

CARLY: You've got a crappy attitude.

CT: So? It's a stupid question! That would never happen anyway. Why are you asking me this?

CARLY: I dunno. I'm bored. It was something to do. Besides, I wanted to know if you could help me.

CT: Help you with what?

CARLY: (uneasy) Okay there's, like, this dude and I haven't told you about him yet.

CT: (surprised) Why didn't you tell me about him?

CARLY: Oh, like you don't know! Every guy I've ever gone out with you've either verbally bashed him or you've physically bashed him to the point where I couldn't even recognize the poor bastard.

CT: I never did that.

CARLY: Oh, please! I can think of about twenty times you terrorized my boyfriends into screaming frenzies.

CT: Name one.

CARLY: Remember Ron Freeman?

CT: No.

CARLY: Well, let me refresh your memory. He was going to take me to the Junior High Graduation Dance last year. But, all of a sudden he remembered he had "something important to do" and had to leave. All after just five minutes of talking to you.

CT: Oh, I see. Well, let me tell you something about Ron Freeman. When you weren't around he turned into mega-pervert and began talk-ing about all the disgusting things he was going to do with you. So, I told him that if he laid one finger on you I would use his face as a dart board.

CARLY: (unconvinced) He said that you told him I was a lesbian.

CT: (thinking for a moment) Was this the Ron Freeman with the long hair, or the Ron Freeman with the really messed up teeth.

CARLY: The hair.

CT: (embarrassed) Oh, him. He was a... He was such a... um, he...That's besides the point! You still shouldn't have kept this from me.

CARLY: So you want me to bring the love of my life home so you can split his face in half.

CT: (surprised) The love of your life!!

CARLY: Give or take a couple years. Now, shut up, let me talk. Okay, I met this guy and he is like the best thing that's ever happened to me but I have no idea how to tell him. (Becoming very solemn) C.T., I think I love him.

CT: (ignoring CARLY's seriousness) Oh, for Christ's sake! I can't believe this bullcrap! What the hell is wrong with you?

CARLY: (angrily) Oh, I'm sorry your highness! I'm sorry I can't control what I feel! And I'm sorry I can't live up to your standards!

CT: But what's wrong with you?! Are you an idiot? You honestly expect me to help you to get a guy that I don't even know who the hell he is. And what's this crap about, "Oh, I think I love him!" What's wrong with you? I thought you were smarter than that!!

CARLY: Well, I'm sorry I'm not as incredibly intelligent as you!! Mister, I -only-date-a-girl-once-in-a-blue-moon! I'm sorry if I can't be over flowing with self control like you!!

CT: Who the hell was the genius who told you that love existed?! Who the hell made you so stupid? Who the hell is this butthead that you're "in love with"? I mean, what the hell is your problem?!

CARLY: (screaming) My only problem is that I'm in love with you!!

(Silence. C.T. takes his binoculars and begins to look out over the audience.)

CARLY: (angrily) Well! Didn't you hear me?

CT: (stunned, tries to cover for it) Um, well. I'm flattered, I really am, but you know based on my beliefs, I don't think it would work out. Besides, even if you did love me, which you don't, you wouldn't have been so blunt about telling me. Also, it's not a good idea for friends to get involved with-(At this point, CARLY lunges forward and kisses C.T. in the mouth. Pause)

CT: (smiles) Nicotine breath. (C.T. kisses CARLY softly on the mouth. Lights down.)

Gallery 37 Literary Program Apprentice Artists and Teaching Artists

Creative Writing Program
Arts of the Living High School
The Guild Complex
Schools Program Spring 1996

Diana Solis, Lead Artist
J.M. Morea, Teaching Assistant

Apprentice Writers
Arnetra Garrett
Katie Barretto
Rachel Chobot
Tamikia Deberry
Maria Gomez
Maria Sandoval
Nancy Sawyer
Nina Wiggins

Creative Writing Program
The Guild Complex
Gage Park High School
Schools Program Spring 1996

Tyhimba Jess, Lead Artist
Lee Momient, Teaching Assistant

Apprentice Writers
Maria Diaz
Shelton Finley
Tony Jackson
Tony Marasas
Lateesha Mitchell
Deonte Mitchell
Charmaye Richard
Sasha Sanapaw
Eddie Thompson
Dontae Walker
Mina Washington
George Wilkins
Charron Williams
Darryle Williams
Keisha Wills

Fiction Writing
The Guild Complex
Downtown 1996

Nick Eliopulos, Lead Artist
Tsehaye Hebert, Lead Artist
Tanya Baxter, Teaching Assistant

Apprentice Writers
Nhat An
Angela Bell
Michael Chung
Susan Ckuj
Jonathan Farr
Hana Field
James Freeman-Hargis
Paul Giedraitis
Colin Harris
Erica Hieggelke
Kevin Irmiter
Ivy Jackson
Sarah Kozlowski
Yadira Lemus
Victoria Maldonado
Margaret McCloskey
Lauren Mizock
Clare Myers
Cristina Ortiz
Shimika Parker
Edward Peterson
Veronica Sansing
Emily Schafer
Pete Steadman
Selly Thiam

Poetry Program
The Guild Complex
Downtown 1996

Quraysh Ali Lansana, Lead Artist
Emily Hooper Lansana, Lead Artist
Glenda Baker, Lead Artist
J.M Morea, Teaching Assistant

Apprentice Writers
Lindbergh Askew
Muneerah Askia
Iesha Bailey
Natasha Binion
Jennifer Clary
Alyssa Coiley
Scenecia Curtis
Onome Djere
Falyn Harper
Taryn Harty
Tajuana C. Herrell
Rachel Jackson
Rufus Jackson
Ann Janikowski
Christopher D. Johnson
Freeda Karadsheh
Eric Komosa
Susan Kurek
Robertha Medina
Nicole Nathaniel
Marija Nikin
Sylvia Pyrich
Michael Roston
Mark Saunders
Sara Shirrell
Lee Skruch
Joann Vergara
Kendra Patrice Walker
Jamaal Webster
Sophia White
Ja-mar Willis
La'Tiffany D. Wriht

Playwriting Program
Pegasus Players
Downtown 1996

Eugene Baldwin, Lead Artist
Felicia Bradley, Teaching Assistant

Apprentice Writers
Natasha Achanzar
Brian Boers
Caryn Bryant
Nicole Conforti
Anthony Evora
Gina M. Holechko
Abbie Kruse
Lauren Mclemore
Dolores Munoz
Brian Norton
Reyna Pena
Yvonne Pitts
Cherisse Richardson
Terrence Sago
Cheryl Thomas
Jason Watkins
Amber Wilson

Creative Writing Program
The Guild Complex
Lakeview High School
Schools Program Fall 1996

Tsehaye Hebert, Lead Artist
J.M. Morea, Teaching Assistant
Amy Ventura, Teaching Assistant

Apprentice Writers
Adriana Berrios
Candace Coleman
Jermaine Gibson
Michelle Hayes
Virginia Hunt
Charles Jaiyeola
Heidi Januszewski
Mark Lopez
Fred Ogundipé
Rachel Ogundipé
Muhammad Ollah
Carmen Peden
Patricia Perez
Robert Prino
Erik Ramirez
Erika Reyna
Jeanette Rusiecki
Ferrari Sheppard
Jennifer Small
Sarah Smith
Arthur Taylor
Thuy Truong
Mohammad Ullah
Alison Ward

Playwriting Program
Pegasus Players
Hugh Manley High School
Schools Program Fall 1996

Rolanda Bringham, Lead Artist
Nambi E. Kelley, Teaching Assistant

Apprentice Writers
Neron Banks
Stacey Brewer
Cornell Brisco
Alicia Cox
Efrien Fry
Tenshia Hawkins
Kenya Howard
Tiffany McDonald
Sheri Members
Richard Moore
Jessica O'Neal
Bryant Robertson
Cornelius Robinson
Rosie Saunders
Emmit Smith
Cory Sorrell
Latisha Straughter
Shermicia Swinney
Keenan White
Romell Williams
James Wilson

Quraysh Ali Lansana

Quraysh Ali Lansana has worked extensively in the Chicago Public Schools since 1990, providing everything from creative writing and visual arts residencies to Black History and Literature curricula. He has led workshops in prisons, public schools and universities throughout the country. His tenure as a Gallery 37 Teaching Artist began in 1992. His first collection of poems,"cockroach children: corner poems and street psalms", was published by nappyhead press in 1995 and a second book of poetry, "walking shoes", is to be published in 1998 by Blackwords/Alexander Publishing Group. Lansana is the Executive Director of Kuntu Drama, Inc., a Black Arts Collective. He sits on the Board of Directors of the Guild Complex, where he also serves as Literary Programming Coordinator.

J.M. Morea

Originally from Flint, MI, J.M. Morea's first manuscript Wish was a semi-finalist in the 1997 University of Wisconsin Press Poetry Series and the New Issues poetry Press Series. A 1996 Pushcart Prize nominee, her work has been published in several literary journals, and has been featured on WBEZ Radio-Chicago. She serves on the Women Writer's Conference Committee of the Guild Complex, and teaches in Gallery 37's Downtown and School Programs.

Eugene Baldwin

Eugene Baldwin's plays have been produced Off Broadway in New York, at the Body Politic Theatre in Chicago, and at regional and community theatres across the country. His short stories and poems are published in various literary magazines. Mr. Baldwin has conducted eighty-five creative writing residencies in the Illinois Arts Council's Artists-in-Education program. He currently teaches at Elgin Community College, Washington Irving School, River Woods School in Naperville, and is a consultant to the Chicago Teachers Center. A host of Eugene Baldwin's high school-age students have been finalists and winners of the Young Playwrights Festival, at Pegasus Players.

Greg King

Born and bred in the Ohio River Valley's "Jewel of the Ohio" Louisville, KY, Greg went on to receive his BFA at the Kansas City Art Institute in 1993. He has regularly exhibited his paintings, prints, and drawings in various venues throughout the states, winning a Professional Assistance Award from the Kentucky Arts Council in 1993 and an Arts Midwest/ NEA Regional Visual Arts Fellowship for painting in 1996. He began his printing/ design business "One Ton Press" in 1994 after having moved to Chicago earlier that year, using it to produce artists books and CD booklets. He currently continues to develop his art, and teaches in Gallery 37's School Program.

Picture Credits

All artwork contained within this book was completed by
apprentice artists employed by Gallery 37.

Contents page: Lisa Munizzi, age 18

Section One:
page 13: Maher Mosa, age 18
page 15: Spencer Baker, age 19
page 17: April Harvey, age 19
pages 18-19: Reyna Nieto, age 20
page 22: Darius Henderson, age 17
page 28: Richard Lidl, age 14
page 31: Xochitl Rivera, age 14

Section Two:
page 38: Oswaldo Maldonado, age 18
page 39: Timothy Santine, age 18
page 40: Trinh Kimngan, age 16
page 45: Katie Fitzgerald, age 14
page 48: Eligha Roberts, age 16
page 50: Xi Peng Mei, age 18
page 53: Sequn Seane, age 16
page 55: Ronald Carrera, age 17
page 59: Kris Eureste, age 15

Section Three:
page 65: Lakesha Jackson, age 20
page 68: Lisa Munizzi, age 18
page 69: Carolina Diaz, age 16
page 73: Xi Peng Mei, age 18

Section Four:
page 92: Sally Situ, age 17
page 104: Nina Wiggins, age 20
page 123: Timothy Santine, age 18
page 129: Chris Beverwyk, age 20
page 143: Jose Torres, age 14
page 152: Joe Cline, age 15

Section Five:
page 188: Darius Henderson, age 17
page 193: Darius Henderson, age 17
page 209: Shenise Smith, age 15
page 222: Nohemi Cabrales, age 16
page 244: Pat Rosen, age 20
page 259: Lisa Munizzi, age 18

Editor's acknowledgements:
Special thanks to
Lisa Key, Development Coordinator, Gallery 37